BÔ YIN RÂ
(J.A. SCHNEIDERFRANKEN)

THE GATED GARDEN
Volume One

THE BOOK
ON
THE ROYAL ART

For more information about
the books of Bô Yin Râ and titles
published in English translation,
visit The Kober Press web site at
www.kober.com.

BÔ YIN RÂ
(J. A. SCHNEIDERFRANKEN)

THE BOOK
ON
THE ROYAL ART

TRANSLATED FROM THE GERMAN
BY B.A. REICHENBACH

BERKELEY, CALIFORNIA

Copyright © 2006 by B. A. Reichenbach
Eric W. Strauss, Publisher & Editor
All rights reserved.

For permission to quote or excerpt, write to:

The Kober Press
2534 Chilton Way
Berkeley, CA 94704

E-mail: koberpress@mindspring.com

This book is a translation from the German of the second edition of *Das Buch der königlichen Kunst* by Bô Yin Râ (J.A. Schneiderfranken), published in 1932 by Kober'sche Verlagsbuchhandlung Basel-Leipzig. The first edition of this work was published in 1920 by Verlag der Weißen Bücher (Kurt Wolff), München. The copyright to the German original text is held by Kober Verlag AG, Bern, Switzerland.

Printed in the United States of America

International Standard Book Number: 978-0-915034-13-1

Typography and composition by Dickie Magidoff

Book cover after a design by Bô Yin Râ

ACKNOWLEDGMENTS

For their continuing generous support
I am gratefully indebted to
Deutsche Bô Yin Râ – Stiftung
Giessen, Germany.

Again for her careful readings
and many thoughtful suggestions
I express my thanks to
Alice Glawe

CONTENTS

Preface........................ ix

Part One
**Light from Himavat and
Words of the Masters**

1 The Luminary's Self-Disclosure
   to the Seeking Soul................ 3
2 The Harvest..................... 13
3 The ONE whose Being is Infinity..... 25
4 Know Thyself.................... 37
5 On the Masters of the Spirit's World .. 51
6 Pitfalls of Vanity.................. 63

Part Two
From the Lands of the Luminaries

1 The Threshold 73
2 The King's Question 97
3 The Pillar in the Mountains 109
4 The Night of Easter 119
5 Communion 135

Part Three
The Will to Joy

1 To All Who Strive Toward
   Timeless Light 147
2 The Teachings On Joy 153

   Epilogue 175

PREFACE

It would be folly to assume that evidence of the profoundest insights of a culture's most enlightened sages might be discovered in the writings of a given people from that culture.

A still greater folly would be the assumption that all one has to do is conscientiously translate all the texts of such a literature in order to preserve the sparks of light entangled in its writings for the benefit of one's own people and its culture.

To be sure, as long as the earth has been circling the sun, all living things have seen its light arising in the East; and from the human beings' first attempts to find their timeless essence in themselves, the most successful of such seekers were natives of the Orient.

Yet of the treasures they uncovered, scarcely fragments ever found their way into the writings of the people from their culture.

As secret knowledge—even for the "sacred scriptures"—were guarded also then the insights that forever shall remain a secret, kept from all who do not in themselves experience what it comprehends.

How readers may acquire this experience, each in ways best suited to his nature, the present book is meant to help them see and learn.

The insights offered in these pages rest upon the bedrock of immutable reality.

Even so, their presentation here is neither an end in itself, nor would it foster "dogmas." It has no purpose other than to offer needed explanations.

Not until the time that seeking readers gained their own experience through these teachings have they truly made this book their own.

Part One

LIGHT FROM HIMAVAT AND WORDS OF THE MASTERS

KNOW THAT
ON YOUR QUEST FOR LIGHT,
YOUR PATH WILL BE PROTECTED
BY THE SPIRIT'S LUMINARIES,
BORN IN THE ETERNAL DAY

CHAPTER ONE

THE LUMINARY'S SELF-DISCLOSURE TO THE SEEKING SOUL

I HERE SHALL TELL you of the way that I myself have gone.

I shall display to you the way I have myself become.

My path had taken me so close to the sun that its fire covered the sky from end to end.

Everything around me stood in flames, both above me and below.

I was a pilgrim on the path into the light and suddenly, without my knowing how, I had myself become the way, nor had I any choice.

But thus transformed into the way, I shot into the goal even as an arrow hits its mark—and in the blazing sun consumed my very being.

That is how I had myself become a source of light and fire.

Consuming my own self within my being's flames, how could my will not want to see that everything were set ablaze and turn to fiery glow!

THE SPIRIT'S suns all burn within the same primordial light.

A self whom fire has transformed into a sun is thus made one with all the other suns and their eternal light.

You do not know the suns whose light my words shed on your path.

Let not your willful mind draw arbitrary limits!

All imagined limits vanish in the Spirit's light.

Seek the light embodied in the suns, and in that light search for the suns themselves!

As a seeker after truth, behold with love, at least a little, the light you see reflected in all radiance.

IF YOU DESIRE to approach eternal light, you must forgo resistance!

THE LUMINARY'S SELF-DISCLOSURE

Everything is still resistance in your being.

Everything within you now still speaks at once—and thus you cannot hear.

Everything within you now still wanders like an aimless eye—and thus you cannot see.

Bid your noisy mind be quiet and let your eye collect its restless search, that silence shall elect you for her dwelling.

In soundless silence only shall you fathom the eternal Word.

Today, however, legions of resisting forces are still at war within you, in endless conflict with opposing hosts.

You have not yet gained freedom in yourself.

You still are not yet truly willing—free of all distracting wishes—to let me guide you on your path into the realm of timeless light.

The "beginning"—eternal Being without end—begets of its own essence the Origin's eternal Light; and that primordial Light in turn engenders the eternal Word.

The Word, however, comprehends the Light of Life, whose radiance shines within the Word that generates the "Father"—the Spirit's Human Being of the Origin—within the silent depths encompassing eternity, which is today the way it always was and shall remain forever without end.

What we make known to you, out of the Word's abundance, is not a fantasy conceived by mortal minds.

It is, instead, disclosure of eternity, not having anything to do with learned speculation.

What you will here receive is Light abiding in the Word.

All of us who sanctioned these disclosures are One within the Word in consciousness and knowledge.

It is our task to bring forth order, rooted in the Spirit, through the Word:—within the chaos of the mirror-like reflections that beleaguer and displace each other upon the surface of continuously churning waves of energy, impelled to strive toward Being's outermost dimensions.

When we teach, we open eyes to show them who we are.

Only through teachings by human example can the Spirit's living light be shown you without blinding your eyes by its infinite blaze.

IF YOU WOULD find eternal light, you have to learn to trust your faith.

Having faith, however, means: unfolding power in order to awaken higher powers.

Even faith expressed in words is able to awaken power, but what you are to learn is not a faith that rests on words alone.

Ultimately, faith is *will*.

According to your faith it shall be done to you as you have willed.

Even as your faith, so, too, shall be your powers.

Only your own power releases all the higher forces which then shall bring you help.

IF YOU DESIRE to encounter light, be sure you learn to pray!

But when you pray, above all else do ask for wings!

Recognize that there are wings which carry you beyond the heights where eagles soar.

Truly, there are wings that let you rise above the farthest stars.

Wings like that you ought to ask for when you pray.

Blasphemy is every other prayer, unless you at the same time also pray for wings.

To all who ask for wings shall truly wings be given.

Your very *will* to fly shall cause your wings to grow.

Even while you pray your soul shall be uplifted.

And now my friend who would find truth, demolish the false gods that cloud your mind, so that you may approach the everlasting One—who knows beside himself no other—the individuated living God within you.

Your God is *in yourself*, and *in yourself* alone can you perceive his presence.

Only *in yourself* can he redeem you with his birth.

And only *in yourself* make you aware that he is near.

You shall not search for "God," save for the God within you!

You should not want to serve nor worship any other "God."

Hear the ancient words that lack of understanding failed to grasp.

Hear them anew, and now with comprehension.

Hear them in your soul and with a trembling heart!

"I"—"am the Lord"—proclaims your God.

"You shall not search for other Gods!"

"You shall not fashion any mental image that it may serve you as a "God," but which would be no more than a pathetically distorted likeness of yourself, existing solely by your will, until the day your life on earth shall end."

You, a seeker after light, here find yourself before all final Truth's beginning and never ending end.

Blest you are if you can fathom what these words would have you understand; words that he who wrote them once heard spoken to him by his God.

Here, I purposely showed you the meaning of these words, begotten of eternity.

CHAPTER TWO

THE HARVEST

LET A PROTECTIVE veil be cast on all the words that have in recent generations been variously ascribed to us.

This will be the wiser course; for many things must still be treated with exceeding care, which we would else be forced to winnow without mercy, if we sought, in all the teachings of tradition, to separate what we have sown from all the weeds around it.

Our spiritually *younger* brothers—and sisters—measure time in ages that, compared to ours, are quite brief.

Some, therefore, felt called upon to make the work that we have to perform move forward at a quicker pace.

How much less would such impetuous promoters without ill intent be pleased with our view of progress if they knew that we today still find ourselves at the beginning of our task and hardly see as yet begun what they have long since written off as finished.

We are sowers spreading seed on land that has been ploughed.

Whether the grains we sow will come to life shall now depend on you.

Be sure you fend off thievish birds that pick the seeds before they can grow roots and sprout!

Protect what is entrusted to your care!

MANY ARE COMPELLED to sit in darkness and countless others live in dreary shade because the days are gloomy—they engulf the light.

But those who will stay watchful, even in the depth of night, shall see the sun at midnight rise and set the sky ablaze.

Helping hands shall come to them and labor in the harvest's work, to gather up the ears of ripened wheat and bind them into sheaves.

Then will shepherds come, arrayed in white, and summon their flocks with the sound of their flutes.

Then shall all who search for guidance find the guide they sought.

That helper then will lead them through the brazen portals to the path across the desert, and toward the towering peaks of Himavat.

Here, the sun is drowned in radiant light and the earth has lost its burden's weight.

Here, the sky is one eternal conflagration and every star burns in its fiery glow.

Everything found ready to be set on fire will here become a flame and vessel of eternal light.

Much, however, still is green and dank with heavy moisture.

And thus it will not burn, but fights against the fire: it quickly grows, then wilts and lastly rots away.

Unerringly will the eternal Fathers select the kindling wood that is to feed the fire's flame.

Star after star they kindle in its radiant blaze.

Know this: to burn, to glow, to shine, or—to molder and decay, one or the other is to be your lot.

If you believe you can escape this fate, you merely are the victim of your folly.

The only power you possess is that of choosing the path you would pursue.

THOSE WHO haughtily regard their mere opinions equal to the timeless wisdom born of God obstruct the work that we are sanctioned to perform on earth.

They denigrate the light illuminating all the earth and sin against the power of the Spirit that sustains their very lives.

Pity the mortal who in this way will sacrilegiously dethrone the Word by idle fancies of his mind!

Before the worlds began, the Word had been in being; and in its essence shone the Light that was the Word's cognition.

Mortals are not able to fathom this cognition by virtue of their thinking; for thoughts are but the servants of the Word.

Whoever would receive the master's radiant gift should bid the servant hold his tongue.

THE TASK THAT we perform is the work of the innermost East: of the Light that imbues the primordial day.

It has been made our task to open souls to living light.

Let those who search for guidance that leads no soul astray preserve our words within their hearts.

We, however, shall be near them, even should they live on the other side of the earth.

We are born into this earthly life as Mediators, sent by the Sons of primordial Light:—by the Fathers who live in the Light of the Word.

Through our mediation has the Light within the Word revealed itself, again and again throughout the ages, in forms that mortal eyes could apprehend and not be blinded.

In mortal flesh and blood we manifest eternal life.

Those who, under our guidance, reach the narrow path that leads to our realm within the Spirit will thus approach their own true selves in the Eternal.

We guide to the Stars of life everlasting, who are in essence one with us—born of the substance of radiant light—abiding in the Light that was in the Beginning, that will forever be, and shall not cease to shine through all eternity.

THOSE OF US who here on earth embody this most ancient unity of wills are very few.

Yet great is our number including all who carried this same burden before our days, and all who shall in future ages have to bear its weight.

None among us is at any time, nor ever could be, separated from the others by attributes of ethnic background, nationality, or language, nor by distances of space and time; still, each one of us retains the physical characteristics of his race.

Within ourselves we worship that which seeks to manifest itself through us.

We have abandoned all things other than the will to be its revelation in the world of physical perception.

Within ourselves we are one absolute identity; and our earthly mortal bodies serve us only as material tools within the world of temporal becoming and decay.

None of us has, in his mortal life, been eager to *attain* what we, without our knowing, long have *been,* and now with conscious knowledge also *are.*

Eternities ago we were selected, by those who are the only ones that can make this selection, and took upon ourselves the duties of the chosen as a sacred, heavy yoke.

Each one of us recalls the day with horror that brought his earthly consciousness the knowledge of the duties and commitments he had already been performing, for millennia, within the Spirit's world before his life in mortal form.

Wherever one of our kind may live on earth, there is the site of one of our spiritual temples.

None of us will offer teachings through his words that rest on no more than his own subjective knowledge.

In the words that any one of us pronounces in his teachings, all the Luminaries of eternal Light are speaking with a single voice.

Futile would be the attempt to sever any one of us from those who are united with him in the Spirit as his Brothers.

Nor could any one of us be separated from the others by his death; for all of us live one within the other, each pervading all, no matter whether we still occupy a mortal body or have returned that garment to the earth.

We left below the sphere of thought and visions and found the realm of primal signs: the world of ultimate reality.

In that domain we dwell and thence pursue our work, unified within our innermost, even though in outer life we would be forced to travel thousands of miles if we wanted to meet in our physical bodies.

A soul that has been spiritually admitted to one among our circle, has thereby entered a temple of the Spirit on this earth.

We seek to reach the hearts of human mortals, so that their souls may find the path into the Spirit, which no amount of mental labor will discover, until the human being's spiritual essence has learned to apprehend it.

To be selected here depends on spiritually sanctioned law, which can be neither bent nor broken.

None among us is at liberty to make himself accessible, within the Spirit's realm, to anyone who so desires.

The river must be near the sea before it can support the ocean's vessels; so, too, the seeker's soul must first have been prepared in order to take up what we have to bestow.

All who spiritually come to us may, to be sure, receive assistance as best will meet their needs; and, in the same way, also guidance in some form; to the extent that such assistance truly will prove helpful, and insofar as they already can discern such guidance, even though it only may affect their outer daily life.

Yet guidance on the highest levels of ascent we are allowed to offer only those whom we encounter after they have reached the end of the path across the desert sands of arid speculation—by virtue of their own resolve.

They alone are destined by eternal law to scale the highest peaks of knowledge in the Spirit.

All others only would be doomed to face a deadly fall if our spiritual guidance sought to lead them on the summit paths, which very few in every generation can ascend.

CHAPTER THREE

THE ONE WHOSE BEING IS INFINITY

W<small>E SURELY WILL</small> not here unveil the vestal purity of timeless truth, whose chosen priests we are in mortal life, nor shamelessly expose its mystery to the curiosity of lusting eyes.

We ourselves will purposely confuse, by spiritual intervention, what mortal minds devoid of calling have from time to time obtained without our sanction or against our will, lest it nourish errors causing harm to those who indiscriminately search for teachings where final truth shall not be found.

After every glimpse of insight surreptitiously obtained by someone without calling we are compelled to fortify the wall of silence that surrounds the sacred shrine; because the

Spirit's law imposes such protection, while we are bound to follow its demands.

You have been given much in ancient and in modern times that did not rightfully belong to those who put it in your hands.

Awake and learn to recognize how thoroughly the Spirit's law will every time destroy again such pilfered gifts, lest what is good from origin become the source of spreading harm.

O<small>NLY FOR THE</small> gifts that we ourselves bestow on human souls do we accept responsibility before the Spirit, that being our duty and appointed task.

Do not assume that in the geographic East—nor even at the foothills of the Himavat, where sacred "swans" have built their nests along the temple building's highest ponds—you might be any closer to the living light of final truth, whose rays illuminate the inner "East," the realm of sunrise in the soul.

Not everything that hails from the external East is, for that reason, light that shines within the Orient of the Spirit.

THE *ONE* WHOSE BEING IS INFINITY

The scorching winds of arid speculation, no less than the infectious fever-breath of rampant superstitions also blow from Eastern lands.

The lowest folly and the highest wisdom have their wellspring in the East.

The light originating in the Spirit's inmost East, however, is everlasting cosmic wisdom.

We have ways of reaching every individual, as well as every people on this earth, directly, without the need for intermediaries.

It solely then depends on those we reach, whether our gifts will be accepted, or shall return to us again, repelled like by a wall of stone.

Seek, then; for thus you shall—be found!

To undertake this seeking, however, you need not even leave your house.

Within yourself alone you ought to seek; and only in your inmost self shall we approach and find you.

Do not believe the self-appointed "mystagogues," who would control your mind and thus pretend to also hold such powers, are capable of doing this.

Nor should you think that we, who are alone entrusted with this faculty, will thereby ever apprehend in you except what stirs your spiritually quickened spark of life within your soul's profoundest depth.

Curiosity is foreign to our nature, and we perceive of you no more than what within yourself is capable of consciously conceiving light.

All our labors have one single aim: to spark and nourish light wherever light is willingly received.

Be sure to guard what we entrust to you!

What we impart is light from the innermost East.

To be sure, the light that is eternal, and shall remain thus through the aeons, brightly shines in all the realms of darkness, but those who dream enamored of the dark do not perceive its rays.

Know this: Today you are no more than your own dream—a dream that is to find and know itself as light within the Word of the Beginning.

THE *ONE* WHOSE BEING IS INFINITY

At no time were you truly in the darkness that your dreaming mind imagined; for whatsoever you perceive as "dark" does not endure within the realm of truth.

Light is what you were from the Beginning, which never will become the *past*, as it remains forever *present*.

T<small>HE WILL TO</small> shine within yourself must animate your being that you may recognize the fullness of your inner light; and thus awaken from the darkness that you dream.

Today you still are but a slave, in bondage to your dreams.

Perhaps tomorrow you already may awaken and your day shall be eternal.

No gloom of night will then deprive your own light of its full abundance.

B<small>Y CHOICE OF</small> your own will—by virtue of your faith in darkness—you let yourself become a dream abiding in the dark.

In the same way it is now your task—by virtue of your faith in light—to make your darkness yield, that light may shine in you and wake you from your dreams.

Be on your guard against your dreams, because the dream-world's powers are tyrannical and zealous to possess you.

They easily could keep you sleeping longer than you should; and, having missed your call, you then would have to wait until another day.

You now still search within your world of dreams, within the lifeless, rigid void beyond the clouds, to find the One who solely will reveal himself in *individuated human spirits*, in countless hosts of *conscious human selves*.

Comprehend: He also dwells in you, and in yourself will say,

"I am within their midst, yet no one hears my words; for my voice is soft, like the song of a bird far away."

L EARN, THEREFORE, to differentiate between the worlds of changing mental notions and the dimension of immutable reality.

What must be overcome is the conceptual *image* of the world; not the world in its *reality*,

THE *ONE* WHOSE BEING IS INFINITY

which would defy the power even of "a god" attempting to surmount it.

If you would learn to apprehend the Spirit's life, endeavor to regain a child's simplicity of heart and mind.

Turn your back on all the "wisdom" based on merely thought.

Flee the phantom worlds you molded merely by your thinking; visions that shall vanish like a baseless spook the day your brain has formed its final thought.

Leave the world of ever changing concepts and ideas, such as it lives and functions solely in your head.

That, truly, is the "great renunciation."

That is the beginning of the path on which the seeking spirit shall itself become progressively transformed to absolute reality.

S<small>ACRED ORDER</small> underlies the law that governs life within the Spirit.

Before the Light proceeding from the Word can reach the hearts and souls of mortals, it first must physically display the colors of the earth.

We, as Mediators, are not primordial Light itself, but Luminaries manifesting that eternal Light.

It is within our essence that the Light of the Beginning assumes the colors of the earth.

Confidently trust the Luminary who, within yourself, becomes your spiritual guide, but in his being solely love the *light* that, flowing through his spirit, desires to approach you.

Let not your soul be clouded by any image of his mortal form if you would be accorded light through him.

What seeks to manifest itself within you is not the mortal self through whom you are enabled to discern the rays of Light, but Light itself, proceeding from the Word.

If you address your inner guide as "master," bear in mind that One alone, in each of us, is finally the *Master* in us all.

WHAT WE ARE we solely have become to bring you help.

THE *ONE* WHOSE BEING IS INFINITY

The Spirit's law demands of us no more than that.

Our task is to awaken energies within yourselves through which your hearts shall be unburdened of all darkness; energies that you possess within; energies of which you must grow conscious if you would learn to master and employ them.

We are to be the guides that lead you to yourselves.

We are to kindle in your souls the Light of the eternal Word.

We are to make the Word reverberate within you.

However, there is nothing we can do for you unless you truly want our help.

Nor are we able to assist you if you do not at least wholeheartedly believe that spiritual help is possible; much as seafarers are convinced that on the ocean's other shore they will encounter land.

We live as mortal human beings, like yourselves, and must as such pay our toll to life on earth like you.

Born to work as mortals here on earth, we truly honor temporal accomplishments.

But we know also that which in itself is perfect; as being the eternal goal toward which all individuations begotten of the Spirit strive throughout the aeons, yet which they are not able ever to attain.

If absolute perfection could truly be attained, all of life would cease the instant it was reached; for only its inherent unattainability imbues all infinite eternities with ever new desire and reason to exist.

The fullness of perfection abides in Him alone who is forever One in numberless Infinity, and who experiences His Being—in infinite configurations within the primal Essence, Light, and Word—unceasingly anew as His Own Self.

CHAPTER FOUR

KNOW THYSELF

Do not believe misguided dreamers if they would have you think that anyone who wishes can become a *Luminary*, a Mediator of eternal Light.

Unfortunately, too many willingly believe each word that flatters their consuming vanity, but in the end achieve no more with all their blind ambition than the destruction of their own unique potential in this life.

Unless one *is* a Luminary of eternal Light from birth—after he, for thousands of years, already *was* within the Spirit's world what also in his mortal life he then must learn to *be*—one shall in vain endeavor to "become" what in the Spirit's realm he has not long since *been*.

Do not strive for that which is not seeking you.

You otherwise might easily fall prey to fatal self-deception.

T<small>HE INDIVIDUALS</small> to whom the realm of nature must unlock its secrets are so extremely rare in every generation that only pathological conceit could harbor the presumption that one might be included in that tiny number.

One who truly is a member of that circle will be conscious of that fact, within his earthly self-awareness, only when the mentor who had guided the unfolding of his consciousness has actively endowed him with the powers needed to perform his spiritual task on earth.

Until that time no human being would be able even for one moment to endure, without disintegrating, the unimaginable weight which, of necessity, would overwhelm his consciousness as a result of the experience that his mortal self-awareness physically embodies an identity that is in fact immeasurably older and had attained its individuated life within the timeless Spirit eternities before his birth.

The writer of these expositions knows they rest on solid ground; even as, since childhood days, he knew himself devoid of all desire to appear important.

Never did he long to be entrusted with the task that he was given.

Yet in the Spirit he had been prepared for its fulfillment, before he had been born; and, having reached his time, the Fathers in the Light of the Beginning found him to be ready, much as on a tree one finds a ripened fruit.

In mortal life he may at times have earnestly sought wisdom, but never would it have occurred to him to strive for occult powers.

Although he did seek guidance in profound humility, he truly never sought the consecration he was later to receive; unaware beforehand that a few are destined for its burdens in their earthly life.

And if he ever heard about such matters, he would dismiss them as mere legends, or as inventions of untamed imagination.

Thus he grew to be a master in being what, without his conscious knowing, he had been from his birth.

Power over occult forces, on the other hand, such as human fairy tale imagination always has ascribed to spiritual mastership, all authentic Luminaries have invariably rejected with contempt, as something one should not by any means desire.

You have been told that there are ways and methods to acquire such uncanny forces?

Truly, it were better for you had you never heard about such things.

Nearly all who strove to gain such powers fell victim to their snares; and pitiable was the fate of those entangled in these traps.

One who is to learn to master occult forces with authority, will first be trained for many years by an empowered mentor, so that he may both safely summon and repulse these energies; and even then they may become his downfall.

The might by which alone such occult forces can be mastered, a power that is gained through long and arduous discipline, demands that one who has grown expert in its use will henceforth constantly employ it; and if his will should falter only once, such failure would disastrously avenge itself.

A single moment's hesitation, or of doubting his own strength, suffices to turn all the forces that his will controls against the one who summoned them, unleashing consequences of immeasurable harm.

Insanity and death from mystifying causes are not by any means the very worst results which thus may come about.

Guilt will then fall on the one who placed such power into hands that were not meant to hold it.

No authentic master in the Spirit would ever risk the burden of such guilt; although he surely knows all practices that may induce such powers in every last detail.

Authentic power in the Spirit ranks infinitely high above occult capacities of any kind.

The pupil, adopted by a spiritual master as his son, must be a mortal in whom the earth's inherent will has "died" and who now lives completely in God's will, in which his spirit has been "born."

The master's only guidance then consists in leading, from the depth of God, and thus to let the pupil use God's will within to make himself its likeness. This, to be sure, may often cause astonishing results.

The world of mortal human beings will then be the adopted son's dimension of activity, while the dominion of eternal Will remains his timeless home.

Those, by contrast, who strive for occult powers, and seek to master them by some external method, have only reached the gloomy twilight sphere of dangerous temptations and desires that destroy.

Magic power in the highest sense—the *Royal Art* of masters unified within the Spirit—is obviously something other than this twilight sphere of dreams

The wondrous force at work within the *Royal Art* is, finally, the will of God's triumphant Spirit, which nothing in existence can defeat.

Mortal man is granted part of this eternal will within his soul as soon as he irrevocably has detached himself from obeying the will of the earth within him.

But those who would no longer serve the will of the earth within them should not assume that, consequently, they now must also "renounce the earth" as such.

Renunciation of the world and earthly life is folly.

Abandoning the world is the narcotic potion of enfeebled souls who think that in this way they can escape their obligations to reality.

By "renouncing" the world you merely chain yourself more closely to the will of the earth; because the impulse prompting your "renunciation" is simply the unsatisfied desire of the earth. It thus is not the Spirit's all-surmounting primal will, whose power all things of its own creation must obey, and which no other force in being can withstand.

You cannot wrest yourself from the will of the earth except by your own will's resolve consistently through action to oppose it.

"Renouncing the earth," by contrast, requires nothing more than indolent passivity.

"To abandon the world" should truly not be counted as an action; besides, in the majority of cases it is no more than the regrettable result of psycho-physical disorders, coupled with the impulse toward excessive self-indulgence.

Foolish in particular are all who treat the *self* with scorn; because they do not know what they disdain.

When they proclaim, "Extinguish *self* within you!" they offer you unsound advice.

Extinguish *self*—and everything in Being is extinguished; for all things in immutable existence, no less than all phenomena, are brought about exclusively by *self* and for the sake of *self;* and only in the *self* can their effects be apprehended.

Nor are you even able to extinguish *self,* however zealously you try to turn your *self* into some selfless nothing.

Actively in Being without end is the primordial *Self* that is begetting you, eternally, out of its very essence.

One would not find you in existence even for a second if the spiritual Will that underlies your being did not—for a millionth of a second—want you to exist.

Say to those who claim that *self* has been extinguished in their nature:

"You did not in reality become devoid of *self*; it merely is your folly that prompts you to believe in this mirage of your imagination.

"You well may have suppressed the *self* that is within you, but you can never bring about its death.

"You failed to understand the teachings of the wise, because a sage is *self* throughout his being, and everything within him is subject to his *self*.

"What you should lay aside, instead, is everything you purely have—assumed!"

As a seeker after knowledge, recognize that *self* is what you are, and have been from eternity, even if you are not yet aware of your identity in the eternal spiral of the Spirit's cosmic order.

Everything—except for *self* as such—is but assumed in time and space.

You well may cling to what you have assumed, defending it as if it were your own; but nothing of whatever you assumed has been your own from your eternal origin.

Everything you have assumed you one day also must again relinquish.

Countless things that you had once assumed have countless times again been taken from you in the past.

Even what you look upon as your "own" body is but a garment you assumed within this world whose essence is—assumption.

Self, however, is your true identity!

Self is one, unique, and indestructible in each of its unnumbered emanations.

It is not possible that any *self* disintegrate.

What has been called the "dissolution" of the self, mainly for the sake of brevity, is in reality a highly complicated process of the gradual destruction of a human consciousness, during which the latter, formerly united with its *self*, becomes detached from it and thereby loses its eternal *self*.

Self can never be explained, nor clarified; for *self* is elemental oneness—"light as such and in itself"—and thus consummate clarity.

Apparent variations in the clarity wherewith the *self* perceives are largely owing to the ebb and flow within the consciousness you witness in the *self*.

Self, eternally begotten of primordial *Self*, remains the everlasting issue of primordial generation.

What you are able to destroy is no more than your consciousness of the eternal *self* within you, whose nature is, however, indestructible.

Yet conscious life within the Spirit you never will attain unless your consciousness gains access to your *self*, such as that *self* embodies life within the Spirit through the aeons without end.

It is within the *self* alone that one can love the *Father;* nor can one love the Light and Word that are in the Beginning but in one's timeless *self*.

And that is what in truth you *are*—you, a *self* that is unique among all other individuations, each alike unique—after you have laid aside all things you merely have assumed.

Do not, then, seek in outer realms what is alive within your innermost alone.

You never shall discover what you seek by searching in the outer world.

Nor shall you ever know what *self* embraces unless you first have sought and found that *self* within your being's innermost.

Yet you will find that *self* within you only if you pursue that search in spiritual sobriety and will not let your consciousness become intoxicated by mirages, conjured up in colorful profusion by your own and other minds' imagination.

Within your being there is only *one* eternal *self*; numberless, however, are the energies, that strive in you for domination by using *self* as their disguise in order to conceal that in reality they merely are assumed.

CHAPTER FIVE

ON THE MASTERS OF THE SPIRIT'S WORLD

What, you wonder, truly is that spiritual community of inner guides and teachers?

How can you reach the helpers who assist you from the Spirit's realm if you are not to search for them in "outer" life?

What purpose is accomplished by these words, which, of necessity, must reach you from "without" if you should not expect those helpers' guidance but in your being's inmost self?

Be assured that, on your quest for light, this spiritual community of helpers is very close to you, although you do not know it.

It guides you from within, and in yourself are you connected with its help, without your even sensing the connection.

In outer life you could spend days and nights together in the same four walls with one who is a *master* in the Spirit's world—as ancient custom calls the Luminaries of eternal Light—yet even then you would not recognize him in his timeless essence; because the One primordial Master, who raised us to be masters in the Spirit, has well concealed our mastership from eyes that are beclouded.

But if with seeing eyes you would approach our spiritual community, be mindful that within yourself you reach the spiritual atmosphere in which we live—we, who learned to see by virtue of the one eternal eye to which no mortal organ corresponds.

You will not apprehend our presence in yourself, however, until the day when for the first time you experience inmost stillness in your soul, undisturbed by wishes, imbued with deepest confidence, and wholly free of fears.

Quiet in your outer life will benefit you little in this quest.

ON THE MASTERS OF THE SPIRIT'S WORLD

The more you will be active in your daily life, the more productively you will perform the work required by your duties, the closer will your inner self be rising to the spiritual atmosphere essential to our being; the sphere wherein alone prevails the quiet no distraction can disturb, which you must seek to make your own.

Perhaps you harbor the romantic notion that we, who have been named "the Lions of Silence," are idle dreamers, otherworldly hierophants, or even "yogis" of the doubtful sort one finds performing in the market place?

Perhaps you think the "Lucid Eyes" to whom the myths of every culture owe insights of sublime reality are priests who celebrate mysterious cults in incense-clouded secret crypts?

You cannot rid your mind of the idea that we are in the service of some earthly human will, or subject, as a group, to a particular religious faith or worldly ideology, committed to seek power?

If you, a seeker after light, would find the path that leads you to the truth you must not let yourself be fooled by the beguiling wealth of your untamed imagination.

Let me tell you that among the spiritual masters active here on earth, some were masters of the sword.

Also know that others once had ruled the fortunes of great lands.

Some of us were working in the arts, some in the fields of science, while others shied away from every kind of art and science, and do so even now.

Some lived among the people of great cities, amidst the worldly turmoil of their day, while others went to dwell in distant, inaccessible seclusion, which even now provides, for nearly all of us, a sacred place of refuge.

In varying ways and situations in the changing course of time can traces of our presence be detected in mankind's history on earth.

We are not, however, spiritually all alike in every way, and each of us retains the freedom to decide whether, and how long, he will remain upon the level he has reached, or whether, and at what time, he is ready to ascend the next succeeding rank.

Yet each of us alike at all times hears the call that summoned him.

Very little would most likely correspond to your exaggerated expectations of the physical appearance of a God-united human being if you perchance were to encounter one of us, whom some have also called the "Masters of the Seven Gates" to God, and if you recognized him in his temporal embodiment.

The outer form, however, matters to the wise as no more than *appearance,* which earthly life requires of necessity. All appearance, to be sure, is in itself deceptive, even though one surely must not judge it a mere "nothing."

And so the "Clouds of Knowing"—sent into a world of manifest appearance—are likewise bound, if they would have the land grow fruitful, to bestow their gifts, in the dominion built upon appearance, by equally adopting garments of *apparent form.*

But do not think that there is need of meeting one of us in person in order to become his pupil in the Spirit.

None of us reveals the truth of final things by teaching "from without."

The words I here address to you may, to be sure, bestir your will to search for timeless truth, but all the insights I can offer in my native tongue are always but a call that would awaken you within; because the wisdom from the Himavat is "taught" in other ways.

Its fundaments reach deeper than what the faculty of mortal comprehension can attain.

Much deeper than all earthly human schools and their forever changing doctrines.

You cannot in your being's innermost abide, however, with those who are the living "stones creating the great wall," before you learned to breathe the air in their domain, high above all seemingly important trivia, and far removed from every merchandizing trick of clever mountebanks.

But even as a sound reverberates on all the harps within a hall the moment when a player's finger plucks a single string, so also shall all sacred sounds be heard by every pupil who was assigned his place within the Spirit's world, after in his soul he had attained the "tuning" of the "harps upon the holy hill."

ON THE MASTERS OF THE SPIRIT'S WORLD

Your inner state of being is the key that will unlock the portal through which you reach the temple's sacred shrine.

Nothing shall be hidden, nor anything be kept from you if ever you have truly found that key. However, it can let you enter only as long as you are able to abide in the receptive state the Spirit's law requires.

But do not strive for seeing visions, nor for hearing sounds—or words as you might hear them spoken from without.

Search yourself and keep your soul awake, lest you become enthralled by fantasies and wishful dreams where you had sought to apprehend reality.

Seek nothing other than your soul's profoundest inner calm, imbued with trusting confidence and undisturbed by wishes.

To the same degree that you approach that inner state you also will draw closer to those who, like yourself, are being guided to the path that leads to truth; and in the same way you will farther move away from them if you neglect continuously to maintain within yourself that state of the profoundest inner stillness that no wish is able to disturb.

No mere external restlessness is able to disturb the inner stillness here described, which is dependent, in yourself, on solely your own conduct.

Do not in your inner twilight search for others whom you feel to be your fellow seekers.

You can merely partake of the energy which they have gained already; and you surely will be able to grow conscious of your own capacities' becoming strengthened in this way, but who your fellow seekers in the Spirit are is known to only him who is your inner guide, no less than he is theirs.

Do not waste time in mental probing, but stay aware that you at all times honestly exert the inner faculties that you already feel you have attained.

You must not let the eye of your soul lose sight of you a single moment.

You else might go astray and would not for a long time grow aware of having left your path to light.

ON THE MASTERS OF THE SPIRIT'S WORLD

If you belong to those who will not lose their time on earth by failing to make use of their inherent gifts, then also you will see the radiant day shine brightly in your soul, already in your mortal life.

You then shall have escaped all dangers; for you will henceforth see your path illuminated by the clarity you gained within.

For now, however, you need not yet concern yourself with that still distant day for whose arrival you must only learn with patience to prepare yourself and wait.

You do not know when you are ready to behold that day; nor is there one who knows.

You alone determine your own time and, thus, it is "your time" you must fulfill.

Let the advice I here can give you be sufficient:

The day your time has been fulfilled, you, too, shall know fulfillment.

All impatience merely clouds your vision, and thus prolongs your inner quest.

Eternal is your inmost self and unto you belongs eternity.

Patiently pursue your inner path!

With calm detachment view whatever you have gathered and "assumed."

You need no more than guard it as a faithful servant.

It is by no means something you possess!

Endeavor every day and every hour to attain the timeless state of inner stillness, even in the midst of the external world's unrest.

Imbue your soul with confidence and faith, and guard yourself against all fears.

You thus approach, within the Spirit's world, the teacher who can guide your inner self; you thus will grow aware, within the Spirit's world, of the sublime community from whose domain he reaches you; and thus you shall at long last find yourself within your Living God.

CHAPTER SIX

PITFALLS OF VANITY

Beware, however, as a seeker after light, of falling victim to your faltering resolve!

Beware, lest you become entangled in the thorny hedge of doubt!

Perhaps you now may almost sense the hidden source from which eternal light arises, even as a wanderer, setting out at night, at dawn may fathom, through the morning mist, the point on the horizon where soon the first rays of the daystar shall appear.

Between yourself, however, and that distant source there grows the thorny, deeply rooted thicket of ceaselessly self-generating doubts.

Eradicate as many as you will, a greater number always shall grow back again.

Do not loose your time with foolish aims!

Never—and though you labored an eternity—would you be able to make progress on your path if you presumptuously attempted first to cut down, branch and root, the thorny hedge of doubts.

Nothing here avails but your unflagging courage.

Pursue your path with energy and firm resolve, even though your feet be bloodied by a thousand wounds of injured vanity.

Unless your feet are pure, the One eternal Master, who is the Lord in each of us, will never let you step on the unsullied crystal stairs that lead to the eternal halls of adoration in the Spirit and the Truth.

Unless they have been cleansed in your own blood, your feet will not be "pure."

Thousands have set out to seek the path to light but let themselves become entangled on the hedge of doubts, because their selfish vanity would not allow them to advance before they had got rid of every thorn.

As an earnest seeker after light, be sure you do not follow their example!

You are protected by your trust in the eternal sun whose light my words embody to illuminate your path.

Insensitive to anything that would impede your stride, reach out to grasp the helpful hands that now you see before you.

In silence walk behind the guide who of his timeless self can say:

"I no longer search for light; for I myself became its luminary.

"I no longer search for peace; for I myself embody peace.

"I no longer search for knowledge; for I myself became the wisdom that endures."

Attribute all things that are good to God.

Do not, however, foolishly presume, as many do, that God must answer every question.

Feel free to ask, and gratefully receive the answer you are given; but bridle your untamed curiosity if all your questions are not answered even while you ask!

The wounds your doubts inflict on you are necessary, for by enduring them your faith will grow in strength.

Do not flee, as cowards do, the obstacle arising on your path; for it is meant to hold you back until you have grown strong enough to continue your pursuit.

Do not presume you are the chosen one to cut and prune the hedge of doubts, both for yourself and others, as vanity might whisper in your ear.

Not until you learn to love your doubts will you be able to guard yourself against them.

Only when no goal you have attained will any longer feed your sense of self-importance will you be judged deserving to reach the highest of all goals.

Your soul must learn to harbor silence if light is to be able to approach her path.

Silence will become your soul's profoundest call for light.

Silently, your soul one day shall then ascend the world of radiance without end.

The better you become at guarding inner silence, the closer you will draw to the insights that your soul desires.

The final insights into the domains of ultimate reality reveal their truth to those alone who in themselves have reached enduring calm, because they learned to foster inner silence.

Yet time and time again, and under countless guises, it lastly is your vanity that undermines your inner calm: by asking endless questions that must remain unanswered until you have attained the stillness no distraction can disturb.

Only when you shall have learned to keep your inner silence will you receive, within your soul's profoundest calm, the answer that shall set your spirit free forever.

Part Two

FROM THE LANDS OF THE LUMINARIES

THERE IS A TINY PORTAL IN YOUR SOUL,
SMALLER THAN A SPECKLE IN A SUNBEAM.

ONE WHO PASSES THROUGH THIS PORTAL
CAN MAKE HIS WAY TO DISTANT LANDS,
YET NEED NOT LEAVE HIS HOUSE.

LONG PAST AGES HE CAN WITNESS
TAKING PLACE THIS PRESENT DAY.

BUT FEW CAN MAKE THEMSELVES SO SMALL
THAT THEY MAY ENTER THROUGH
THIS TINY GATE
IN FULLY LUCID CONSCIOUSNESS.

CHAPTER ONE
THE THRESHOLD

Having arrived at the temple where he would receive his consecration, the pupil asked his master,

"Allow me one more question, master, embodiment of certitude, into whose hands I now have put my trust these many years: How, through your own eyes, do you see yourself, knowing what you know about your timeless nature? You, whose power masters everything within you and whom no other power any longer can control?

"Is the being that you are still given in man's earthly nature or have you found within you something else, which uses the material human body only as a mask?"

And the master replied,

"I am, like you, a human being; yet what I was *before* my mother gave my earthly body life and limb, I here did not become until the day I overcame the sleep that holds the human mortal on this earth.

"Only after I had learned to overcome the earth-engendered sleep in which the human mortal of this earth is satisfied to dream his life, was I made master, also here on earth, of my eternal powers.

"If, then, you ask me what I am, all I can tell you is,

"I am—my Self, and nothing other than—the Self I am."

"You are your *Self*?" the pupil stammered in confusion.

"Your *Self*?—"

"How am I to understand your words?"

"My dear pupil, ever thirsting after knowledge," said the master in reply, "how much have I already told you, and how much more do I still have to tell you! And yet, how many things must I forever keep from you unless you first can name them for yourself.

"Will you know much more about me if I say,

"I am my timeless powers' master; for I became their primal force of self?

"They now are conscious of themselves within me, and in my will alone they know their own existence willed."

"Tell me, then, about the powers whose primal force of self you are, you sage of mighty soul!" the pupil asked his teacher.

And the master answered,

"Hear and comprehend within your heart, you seeker after timeless light.

"When you mortals, in your state of waking sleep and in your earthly way of understanding say, 'we see the world with our eyes, we feel it by our touch, and we perceive its presence through our senses,' you speak of no more than a small part of reality, which you are able more or less to apprehend.

"I, however, know the whole of Being and consciously discern it as I live.

"I see, I hear, and also feel more than you mortals do.

"I live in all dimensions of reality, which is composed of countless worlds like yours and in itself comprises all existence.

"Interwoven, penetrating one another, all dimensions of reality expand within the self-same space.

"Hidden in your earthly world, concealed behind that world's material forms, abides the realm of spiritual energies whose primal force of self I am within the Spirit.

"These forces manifest their nature as primordially creative elements; but, at the same time, by virtue of creating, they likewise work destruction.

"On their own, they are inert and powerless, because they lack the impetus to manifest their powers by themselves. The primal force of self, however, which is at work in one who truly is himself, imbues them with the impulse to experience their existence, and thus they turn into dynamic elements by virtue of the Spirit's will.

"The impact of these powers is felt by all who live on earth—by kings and beggars, by rich and poor, and strong and weak—yet hardly any have an inkling of the worlds from which this influence affects their lives.

"It is concealed to nearly all; for in their mortal bodies they only dream they are awake, the while their souls are fast asleep.

"But also hear what else I have to tell you, given you are to become an eye that sees the Spirit's worlds.

"Interwoven and immersed within the world you mortals take to be the only universe, and likewise integrated with the world whose elements are living fire—the one whereof I told you here—there is a world of purest light, transilluminating all dimensions in existence and revealing them within itself.

"These three distinctive worlds, embracing and pervading all in radiant self-experience, the Mighty One sustains who in His name knows no one but Himself.

"To us He is revealed in silence.

"Within Him and by virtue of His Being lives each one who has become an eye that sees all worlds in being.

"It is He that made the primal force of self the queen who rules the elements of living fire.

"In truth, you likewise could say 'She' when speaking of that Mighty One; for in His nature 'male' and 'female' are enclosed.

"At the primordial beginning of the individuations, who here on earth regard themselves as 'human' beings, the spiritual human self, as the eternal procreation of the 'Father,' was in possession of the primal force of self and thus had been the master of all the forces of the living fire.

"Yet when the elements of that dynamic fire, which burns without a flame, revealed their might in all domains of life to the primordially begotten human spirit, he lost awareness of the primal force of self within him, to which alone the fiery elements owe all their greatness, energy, and power, and—shrank from them in fear.

"The human being's primal guilt is fear; for fear alone, inspired by the forces that were subject to his will compelled the human spirit, begotten of the Origin, to fall from the eternal realm of light.

"You now have learned the cause of all the evil present on this earth.

"Not the human being only must now endure and suffer evil, but no less all the other worlds to which the fallen human spirit brought the fear by which he first was overcome.

"You stand in awe before the 'wonders of creation,' quite unaware that everything you apprehend originated in your spirit's own eternal will—which here on earth is paralyzed—and would display far greater wonders yet if the dimension you call 'nature,' to which you in this life are yoked, could now still recognize you as its master.

"But all the forces in that realm must of necessity continue working as before, like wheels keep running in a clock that has been wound.

"Nor is there anyone but you alone who also can *redeem* that realm of 'nature,' even though a million years might pass before you do.

"Do not assume, however, that only this small planet, on which we live here now, must by itself bear all the consequences of your 'fall'!

"The entire physically experienced universe with all its suns and planets has man alone condemned to being without 'God' as a result of falling from the consciousness of his own spiritual power; for only to the human spirit's care had been entrusted, from the Origin, what unseen powers' greed to rule, unconscious of all spiritual life, today has conquered as its own domain.

"Uncounted multitudes of life are now condemned—though innocent—to suffer for the human being's guilt.

"Guilty, the human being doomed his own existence here on earth to be a life of grief and suffering.

"And only by the human being, who once had out of fear abandoned his primordially invested power, can all of suffering creation one day again be wrested from the grip of its tormentors, who feast upon the untold pain the human spirit's fall from light was fated of necessity, without intention, to unleash.

"Now hear what else I have to tell you about the human being's destiny, which could not be averted even if originally a single human spirit only had succumbed to it.

"Continuously bringing forth new evil, it courses through the ages and countless human lives, increasing fear—the guilt engendered at the origin—in each succeeding generation.

"And so the human being fell from both his spiritual power and the greatness granted him in God, sinking ever lower, until he saw the last hope of recovering his self-awareness by entering an animal's material form.

"The creature you call 'early man' became the animal the human being, begotten of the Spirit —the former lord and master of the earth— selected as his dwelling after having 'fallen,' overwhelmed by fear, from his primordial state of unity with God.

"Even so, the power from on high did not entirely desert the fallen self.

"Alive through energies abiding in the Origin, its rays pervading the material creature body —hidden in the animal, and in the animal concealed unto itself—the mortal human vaguely senses still the primal force of self within him as if it were a being of a strange and higher kind.

"The animal became the *refuge* of the fallen spirit in his exile without home, because his home no longer recognized the stranger, and thus the body of the mortal creature also would become the *cave* of his *salvation*.

"The moment when the primal force of self begins to shine in him, his soul rejoices in the animal he occupies and all the creature's burning drives grow pale in this immortal light.

"Vehemently then he longs for that eternal light within his creature body, and growing zeal impels him ever closer, after each new ray he apprehends.

"A FEW AMONG the individuations that here on earth now use the name of 'human' beings —their courage strengthened by having witnessed, from the Spirit's world, the anguished toil in animal existence, a fate they were to undergo as well—pursued the light with such determination that it was able once again to reach them: before their birth into this mortal life.

"On them the primal force of self once more bestowed itself and thus became their own.

"They were the first among the helpers of their fellow mortal brothers and sisters, who lived asleep in animal embodiment.

"They became the seeing eyes of all the worlds.

"They master and control the forces of the living fire, which serve their will with fiery zeal.

"Do you *now* know what I am?" the master asked, concluding his instruction.

And the pupil, bewildered as if awaking from a dream, replied,

"Yes, Lord and Master, I think I now can vaguely fathom what you are.

"But kindly still explain to me—seeing that you have made clear so much already to my understanding—was it your father to whom you owe that power in the Spirit, or was your mother's body the source that granted you such insights?

"Forgive me if my question seems to ask for more than you are willing to explain.

"You know I bow before you in profoundest veneration, and yet my eyes will not allow me to forget that they perceive you merely as a human being, in appearance just like other mortals, and that they search in vain to find in your external form the earthly cause of your enlightened knowledge."

"Oh, what a simpleton you are!" the master replied, "I expected you were asking about *me*! I thought you wanted to know what *I am*.

"Instead, you asked about the mortal creature that here still serves me as material food, a body I consume by living in this world, sustained by its potential.

"The source that gave me what my words have offered you, you heard me speak about again today.

"You, however, do not hear what you are told, because you still are spellbound by the sleep in which you mortals dream your lives in thought.

THE THRESHOLD

"Know that what my words disclosed to you is knowledge rooted in the Light of the Beginning, and that such knowledge is attained by none in whom the primal force of self is not alive.

"But now it is your turn to tell me what *you* are; because the law demands that, in this sanctuary, any question you ask me, I then must also put to you.

"What, then, are you? Given that you still are mastered by so much and yet have learned to master but so little?"

AND THE pupil replied,

"Master, the question you ask me with such scornful words is one that, I believe, no one but you could answer.

"I myself—I do not know."

And the master said,

"No human ever was as bold as you!

"How could you dare to set foot in this temple—this shrine from which no one escapes who has no answer to my question—if you cannot even tell me what you are?

"Wretched nothing! If you are not wise enough to know the answer, let my question stir at least your wits, lest these walls be forced to witness your destruction!"

Barely able to control his voice in his emotions' turmoil, all his body trembling as he spoke, the pupil now responded,

"How can you, whose love embraces all, allow your pupil to be killed, merely because he has no answer to your question?

"Perhaps I truly am no more than *nothing*—as you say—although your word may veil a hidden sense."

"Foolish you!" the master continued in an icy voice of mockery, "You are *nothing*, not merely in some hidden sense, but in the common meaning of the word!

"I see *nothing* on which I could bestow the final consecration, which each of us has been conferring on another, ever since the first among us had received it through the Word of the Beginning from the essence of primordial Light.

THE THRESHOLD

"I see before me *nothing* worthy to be consecrated as long as you still do not know what finally you are.

"A moment past, I saw my pupil stand before me.

"Now I look at and I speak to *nothing*."

Hearing this, the pupil screamed like one in agonies of fever,

"Master! My teacher! You hold your pupil in contempt!

"You want to see me perish and destroyed!

"You never spoke to me this way before!"

"You *know* who stands before you!

"You *know* exactly what I am!

"You know I would not stand before you now had you and those who are your kind not called on me to serve you!"

"What nameless thing here dares so boldly to denounce me?" the master uttered with contempt.

At that the pupil's voice made all the walls reverberate within the sanctum's darkness as he yelled,

"I AM the one who spoke! But I did not denounce you!

"I AM he—your pupil!

"The one who stands before you now is I MYSELF!"

Having screamed these words with all his might, the pupil's consciousness deserted him and, all but lifeless, he fell to the ground.

AFTER A LONG and heavy sleep, at last he finally awakened.

Before the bed on which his nearly lifeless body had been laid now stood the master.

The pupil looked around but could no longer recognize the room; for now he found himself within the temple's inner halls.

But then he recognized the master and saw that his face was radiant with joy.

"Rise," said the master in a voice that showed his love, "Rise, and scale the first of the seven steps that lead you to the temple's inmost sanctum.

"There you shall attain the power which the fiery elements of Being must obey.

"You now have passed the trial of the threshold; for every fiber of your being for the first time was transfigured by the Word.

"Before, only head and heart had been alive in you.

"Now, in your scream of terror in the face of death, everything within you came to life.

"Now the human spirit in the mortal creature has awakened as a conscious self and thus has overcome the creature's sleep."

THE PUPIL heard these words and hardly could believe what had occurred.

Still half in doubt he took the master's hand and said,

"How unmeasured is your kindness, Master, and how compassionate your heart! What can I ever do to thank you?"

Yet the master merely shook his head and answered with great calmness in his voice,

"Ascend the steps!

"And if you have the strength to meet the task the way it must be met—the two of us shall meet again.

"Whoever has attained the readiness to find—here he shall be found.

"But if you came too soon, you shall not even now escape from these unyielding walls.

"Farewell!

"Perhaps—we are to meet again.

"The last ordeal still lies before you!"

Having said these words, the master led his pupil silently through dark and winding, endless passageways, and when they had arrived before the seven steps, he silently withdrew.

Alone—denied all help—the pupil had to try to scale the seven steps.

His powers firmly concentrated in an iron will, after endlessly repeated fruitless efforts, he finally succeeded in ascending the height of the initial step.

Each succeeding step proved still more difficult to scale than those he had already mastered.

Many times he felt his powers threatening to fail him.

The seventh step, however, could scarcely be ascended, because its height was equal to his own.

Drawing on his last remaining strength, the pupil had to struggle to surmount himself, until he finally succeeded, after agonizing efforts, to raise himself onto this highest step as well.

Here at last the way into the temple's inmost sanctum lay before him free and open.

Having arrived at the temple's sanctum, the pupil here found all assembled who before him had surmounted the same demanding steps, and in their midst he also recognized the master who had taught and guided him.

Catching sight of him, he gratefully wanted to kiss the master's hands; for clearly he could feel the transformation that had taken place within him and that he now indeed possessed the power which his master had assured him he would gain if he were able to ascend the seven steps.

But the eldest of those assembled in the temple's sanctuary desisted with a kindly gesture, saying,

"Whom could you any longer thank—except the One eternal in whose name you have become a Word?

"Understand, we all are one identity within the One who comprehends us all.

"Within you was what called us to approach you.

"Within you was what strove to find its timeless self.

"Within you was what now has been perfected in yourself.

"You henceforth live in us, as we now live in you.

"We—a single body unifying all—in turn live in the One in whom we are united.

"Knowing Him we worship His identity—within ourselves."

AND THUS the pupil had himself become a master and now was one with all who earlier had been his guides, having found him readied to accomplish the eternal union—before he had been born on earth.

CHAPTER TWO

THE KING'S QUESTION

"Explain to me, Immortal One," the king addressed the sage, "why every wise man's wisdom differs from all others.

"Each one of them proclaims his teachings as the truth, yet what they teach is not at all alike."

"They all convey the self-same truth," replied the one who was believed to have attained the all-embracing union, which makes those who have reached it *one with all of being,* so that they can no longer be in conflict with themselves and thus become inseparable from the knowledge of the everlasting One within the origin-begotten Light.

"Forgive me, Venerable Teacher, if I am forced to contradict you," the king responded to this answer.

"I have savored the teachings of many sages and the taste of every doctrine was quite different.

"One teacher spoke of many corporeal births of the same individual life in many different bodies, each born anew after the loss of the previous one; another, however, knew instead of many births in the realm of the soul, but only in a single mortal body, granted merely once, and in the course of no more than a single life on earth.

"One looked upon the gods as judges, the other saw the human being standing far above all gods; and according to such teachings, a self that has attained perfection had powers even to command the gods.

"How can you reconcile such contradictions?"

"All such teachings speak about one single truth," the sage replied.

"But how," the king objected, "can all these doctrines teach such different things if in the end they all contain the same eternally unchanging truth?"

To that the sage made this response:

THE KING'S QUESTION

"Allow me, Mighty King, to answer your question with a parable.

"On a radiantly sunny day a master was sitting with his pupils at the shore of the ocean.

"Not one wave disturbed the endless mirror of the sea and the dome of the sky gleamed like a jewel cut from a single stone.

"And so the pupils asked the master to join them in a boat that they might row with him into the distance of the endless sea.

"The master climbed into the spacious vessel and the pupils plied the oars until the land had vanished from their sight.

"Then, as they rested, shielded from the sunlight by a sail, the master said,

'I shall test you, by way of your own words, to discover whether you in truth already see the things my teaching strives to make you see.

'Tell me, then, what is it that you see?'

"Now the first of the pupils observed his reflection on the unstirred surface of the water and vividly admired how faithfully the ocean mirrored his appearance.

"The second searched across the waves and found their limit where the dome of the sky defined the ocean's depth and, knowing well that even at that distant point he would behold the same unlimited horizon, his heart was lifted by the sight of such immeasurable vastness, so that in stirring words he reverently praised Infinity.

"And when the third one came to speak, he dwelled upon the school of fish that swarmed about the vessel in the deep clear water and he lovingly described their fluid forms and the irradiant glitter of their many-colored scales.

"And in this way each one described a different view, and yet they all spoke from a single place.

"When finally the fourth one had paid tribute to the light whose rays embellish everything and, enraptured by its beauty, had audibly extolled in chosen words the praises of the flaming orb to which all light upon this planet owes its being—the pupils looked expectantly at their master; and the three who had spoken earlier now felt certain that only the fourth had given the answer the master expected.

"But the master said,

'I see the sun and I see the light; I see the apparently endless expanse of the ocean; I see the creatures of the deep that throng about the shade of our boat; and I also see myself reflected in the liquid mirror—but I see also more, and more than all of that I want to teach your eyes to see.'

'Do tell us, Venerated Master, what other things beyond all those you see!' the pupils now entreated with one voice.

"Yet the master responded,

'Have I still not talked enough about it to you even now?

'For many months already I have told you of the thing I see, and still you do not know what thing I speak about?'

"At this they all exclaimed,

'Never before have we been together with you on the ocean, Master, and yet you say that you have told us what you see?'

'Did I say I had told you about the ocean, or did I rather speak about the thing I see?' replied the master and then continued his monition with these words,

'You rowed me out onto the sea and assumed I wanted you to tell me about the ocean, of the vastness of the waters, and of the light wherein all things are bathed.

'The sea, however, expresses itself, and so do all the things we see about us.

'If here I were surrounded by a thousand pupils in their boats, my ears would have been filled with a thousand narratives of ocean, light, and of infinity, made audible in words of human tongues.

'Yet would it be any different in a grove of palms?

'Or on the snow-capped summits of the Himavat?

'Groves and mountains, too, have voices to express themselves, and so I have no need to turn to you if I would hear them tell their tales.

'What I, instead, had wanted you to tell me of was that which I see everywhere and always, even though it lies beyond all time and space.

'One who can see that will then no longer listen to what sky and sea, nor groves or mountains have to tell.

'You, however, still seek in the outer world because your inner realm has not yet seen the sun and, thus, remains in darkness.

'But once you shall be *kings* within yourselves, everything that lies without must come to you and pay you tribute whenever you demand.

'Be satisfied, therefore, to let all things that lie without tell of themselves in their own tongues, and hear them as you would, but ask no questions for which you at this time will not receive the answer from without.

'Wait, then, until you shall be masters in yourselves, so that one has to give you, in the realm outside, whatever you demand; for if you go into the world as beggars, one only gives you handouts as one pleases.'

"Having heard these admonitions, the pupils felt ashamed and were silent, each pondering the master's words in his heart.

"But as the evening now approached, it was decided briskly rowing to return to shore; and with each stroke the pupils vowed, before their asking any questions about the world outside, above all else to strive for mastery within."

"IN VIEW OF that," the king remarked, as here the sage had concluded his parable, "it would appear that only those who still see matters from 'without' continue to show differences in their teachings?"

"And so it is indeed, Great King," replied the one who had attained perfection, "yet bear in mind that even those who manifest their inner world, after having gained true mastery within, can only speak in their own tongues.

"If you would know the truth as you alone can apprehend it, you need to search for it within yourself!"

AS NOW THE king said nothing more, the sage rose from his seat, aware he was no longer needed, and passing through the court's attendants went his way, immersed within his inner light.

The king, however, pondered in his mind whether he should not himself become a seer knowing truth.

But after a while he put his thoughts to rest, saying to himself,

"Who can be sure that I would find the truth within me?

"Can one, indeed, be even certain that truth has not abandoned me already long ago, because she felt I had abandoned her?

"Why, besides, should I be forced to face the truth and look her in the eye?

"Perhaps I would not even be assured of my own truth! How, then, should I be able to determine what is truth?

"Furthermore, so many sages live throughout the lands I rule and everywhere one finds enlightened teachers.

"To me, their king, they must reveal their purest wisdom, and I can then select the things I like.

"My forebears, too, would not accept as truth except what suited them, and that same privilege I shall claim for myself."

And that is why this king remained deprived of knowing truth until his end.

CHAPTER THREE

THE PILLAR IN THE MOUNTAINS

THE PUPIL, whose home was in the western world, far from the towering mountain range upon whose slopes the master lived, had just been asking about the venerable teacher of Nazareth and sought the master's guidance.

"In my native land," the pupil explained, "there are many famous scholars who do not think this teacher ever truly lived on earth and they believe his features had been formed by legends; some, indeed, are of the view that the reports about his life are nothing more than veiled accounts of astral myths, supposedly held sacred by cults in ancient times.

"But you, a source of purest light, have many times said words to me which, I believe, you drew on purpose from the narratives that tell about the life and teachings of this Jewish master.

"You spoke with reverence when you mentioned his name and, if I understood your words correctly, you rank him higher than all others that ever scaled the path to all-embracing oneness.

"Why, I wonder, do I not find you as well among the faithful who profess themselves believers of that Jewish master, whom even you hold in such high esteem?"

The pupil sought an answer to that question because he still was unaware of Him who ultimately is the "Master" in every master born within the Spirit.

Y<small>ET THE GUIDE</small> to whom these words had been addressed merely listened with an understanding smile, but did not break his silence.

And so the pupil, having doubts about his question, feared it might have been improper and, not quite knowing what to say, continued,

"Doubtless, you are right to find my question foolish, given that you master spiritual forces of whose reality my teachers in the West knew nothing.

"Surely you must look with pity on us people in the West!

"Yet even so, I ask you to regard at least this single question worthy of your answer,

"Would it not be better for us people in the West to leave that Jewish master's teachings be and rather treat them like an ancient myth that nowadays has nothing more to tell us?

"Every age has, after all, its own approach to seeking truth, according to its needs and circumstances."

While the pupil was saying these words, the master stood still.

On their walk the two had reached the height of a plateau that separated the waters of two rivers.

The place where they stood was marked by a mighty square pillar of stone, hewn from a single rock in ancient times; each side bearing a flat surface.

Deeply carved into the rock, in the country's native script with letters of majestic size, the pillar bore the sacred syllables: OM MANI PADME HUM, signifying, "Truly, the lotus blossom bears the secret."

And underneath those words one saw a sign directing foreign pilgrims toward their journey's destination.

"Don't you think," the master remarked as if he, lost perhaps in his own thoughts, had failed to hear the pupil's question, "Don't you think it would be better that this old colossal pillar vanish from this site?

"I have seen different road signs among the nations of your race, and I intend to work toward having one of those contemporary novel signs brought up here from the city in the south, attractively painted and adorned with sundry decorations, such as your people in the West so skillfully create these sign posts in cast iron.

"Let the pilgrims see that the monks in the monastery here below us are not so thoroughly detached from the world that they no longer can keep pace with the times.

"One then may topple this outmoded pillar, which long has been unsuited to the age, and let it crash to pieces in the gorge below the pilgrims' road.

"After all, what could this chunk of rock have possibly to tell us in this day and age?"

"Surely, master, you cannot mean what you are saying!" the pupil responded in shock.

"It is true, one can tell the pillar is old, but it displays the great and simple forms that do not age at any time; and the sacred syllables are carved into its surface in letters of such beauty that one will hardly find their equal.

"How could you ever let this mighty work, this witness of majestic dignity, be ruined and replaced by such a garish road sign of cast iron, utterly devoid of taste and grandeur, of the kind that one today, regrettably, must see on every street?

"How could you look upon the sacred syllables with such indifference that you might bear to see them painted on such wretched, gaudy varnish?

"Besides, at heights like these, exposed to all the elements, that sort of thing would very soon corrode.

"This pillar, on the other hand, hewn from a single rock by sovereign skill, has stood here longer than a thousand years; and it may still, for many thousand years to come, serve as a beacon to all pilgrims, who can see it clearly from afar, and thus direct them toward the temple. Indeed, this pillar is itself a sacred work and worthy to be honored as the godhead's shrine.

"Surely, what you said was not in earnest; for how could everything that argues here against what you proposed be hidden from your insight, even for a moment! From you, to whom all human feelings are revealed!"

Here again the master only smiled but did not say a word, just as he had done before.

Then the two continued on their way.

Silently they walked down to the valley, toward the far-spread buildings of the ancient lamasery, close to which the master had retired.

The pupil, however, thought about and wondered why his master always sought a way to make him answer his own questions—even as he had done here again, when asked about the Master of Nazareth.

CHAPTER FOUR

THE NIGHT OF EASTER

THE BATTLEMENTS and towers of the city, famed for its ancient temple, shimmer in the full moon's brightness like tracings etched into the radiant air.

The valley's wide expanse is flooded by silvery light, which lies upon the barren heights of the Judean Mountains like a veil of glowing hoarfrost.

We find ourselves some distance from the city's walls and here we see an olive grove before us.

Like a cloud of grayish green it seems to nestle at the steep decline of a hill.

But close to the vertical face of the rock there has been planted a row of dusky, solemn-looking trees—one can tell that human hands have placed them in this way—and now they strive to rise above the cloud of heavy gray-green foliage like a watch of guardians shielded by black armor.

All things rest in total silence.

But did there not just now appear a figure, clad in white, near the edge of the olive grove, where lucid shadows separate it from the open field of asphodels?

Indeed! One sees that there is something moving.

A human form!

A figure robed in white now cautiously steps forward, lifts an arm above his head, probably to shield his eyes from the glare of the moon, and carefully scans the open surroundings.

Nearby one sees a road that winds its way into the mountains.

Resembling a shiny rope, inadvertently dropped, it lies upon the ground.

The eye can easily follow the road until, at a moderate height, it disappears behind obtruding rocks.

THE NIGHT OF EASTER

The searching figure looks in all directions, but he apparently finds nothing to alarm him.

He now steps back again into the bluish shadows and disappears among the olive trees.

What could he have been doing there?

But then one recognizes the sudden gleam of something white again; only now there must be more than one; for white reflections show and vanish at the same time here and there among the twisted branches of the olive trees.

One of them just now steps out into the open.

No—there is another.

They are carrying something.

Apparently, it is a heavy, precious burden.

Lastly then two more come into view and now one can see very clearly that the weight the four are seeking to secure and shelter with such care must be a human being or, perhaps, a human being's body.

He, too, is wrapped in white, like them.

Whatever could have happened here?

Silently they have already crossed the field of asphodels and reached the open road.

And here one can see still more clearly that they are carrying one of their own.

But he must be dead.

Under his knees they have tied a length of cloth that reaches over the shoulders of the two that walk in front.

Each of them is holding the twisted canvas stretched across their shoulders with both hands; and the weight they carry is a heavy strain.

The two who walk behind support the dead man's upper body; they are reaching around his back and under his arms.

His head appears to rest between their shoulders.

Walking is made very painful for the four.

Only very slowly are they moving forward.

After having for some time continued on their way, becoming less distinctly visible to our eyes, one can see them cautiously pausing to rest.

THE NIGHT OF EASTER

It may also be that once again they warily examine the surroundings; yet even while they pause, they carefully keep holding the body they carry, having belonged to one of their own, in the same position as they had before.

They must have loved him deeply when he was alive.

No one unloved is carried with such care.

Their way of holding him bears witness to their reverence.

THEY HAVE resumed their journey and moved on.

Now they are quite close already to the mountains.

All one still can see of them is something white that slowly makes its way; not having followed them before, one hardly would be able to detect them any more in the reflected brightness of the road.

Now they turn and move behind the rocks that hide the road from view.

Nothing more is left of them to see.

Moonlight wraps the landscape like a veil of glittering silver.

Everything appears again as if no one had ever used that road.

SUDDENLY, ONE hears a furious shout; it comes from where the row of dusky trees has grown above the olive grove.

More angry yelling follows—it sounds like irate soldiers cursing—and in the darkness flickers the reddish light of torches that, together with the uproar, quickly fades in the direction of the city's walls.

One could see the torches only while their glow moved past the dark face of the rock and along the row of dusky trees.

Then their light was swallowed by the moonlight's glare.

Now one recognizes nothing more.

From here, one cannot see the road to the gate of the city; otherwise one should be able to detect the torches again in the shadows of the city's wall.

YET ON THE barren hill of shards outside the city one recognizes that three crosses have been raised.

THE NIGHT OF EASTER

On two of the gibbets the bodies of the crucified appear still visible, but the third cross seems to be empty.

Indeed, one can see very clearly it is bare.

Why, everything this night appears as bright as day!

But to what purpose has that cross been raised?

Someone, surely, must have hung upon it!

But why, then, was he taken down?

Could it have been the one whom the mysterious figures clad in white had borne away?

But in that case he must have perished quickly; for the condemned will sometimes hang up there for days on end as if already dead, till suddenly they howl again like savage beasts and one can see their end has not yet come.

Perhaps it was a victim who could not bear much pain, or had already nearly died from the abuse inflicted by the Roman horde before they hanged him on the cross.

But for what reason was he taken down?

At the olive grove, all is quiet once again.

Let us go there and discover what had been the cause of the disturbance.

Everyone by now has surely left the site.

But this is not, as we had thought, an olive grove!

It is, instead, the open garden of a wealthy man.

Approaching on good footpaths we have already reached the row of dusky trees.

Over by the sheer face of the rock, there seems to be some kind of cavern hewn into the hillside.

Indeed, there is—and now we see the cavern is a tomb!

Where we stand it is dark because the moonlight is obstructed by the hillside and we have neither torch nor lamp.

The cavern appears to be quite deep; still, one dare not try to go in very far, for fear of plunging into some hidden abyss.

But coming toward us there again is such a figure robed in white!

Who might that be?

Most likely the owner of the garden!

Yet what could he be doing here this hour of the night?

"Are you of those that seek the one who had been buried here?"

"No, we have not heard of anyone who is supposed to have been buried here; we merely saw four figures, garbed in white like you, who carried a body from this garden toward the mountains; and then we heard loud noises coming from this site and saw the glow of burning torches."

"Guard, then, as your secret what you were granted to behold; but be assured that he whose body you saw being carried from this tomb, although he did succumb to torture, is even now alive."

"We earlier observed that on one of the three gibbets at the hill of shards there had been no one hanging; yet someone must have hung upon it. Was it perhaps the one of whom you speak?"

"It was the same, indeed! And he is my Brother; and likewise those you have seen carry him are his Brothers, as also they are mine."

"But why, then, was he put to death? You truly do not look as if you were the brother of a murderer or robber!"

"Because he liberated humankind from death, for which the subjects of eternal death exacted vengeance."

"Your words are strange to hear and pass our understanding; even so, the way you speak impels one to believe you."

"But what explains the noise we heard a while ago?"

"Those were the guards we put to sleep by magic means, so that we could remove our Brother's temporal remains, which briefly rested in this tomb at the request made by a wealthy friend, and granted by the one who holds the power in the city.

"They had been ordered to protect the tomb; and when I woke them up, as if I were just passing by and did not know why here they

THE NIGHT OF EASTER

lay asleep, they lit their torches and discovered that the opened tomb was empty.

"That provoked their angry cursing.

"Now they are searching in the city for those who might have opened the tomb; because they want to recover the body.

"I, however, shall stay here for a time to comfort the Brother's friends and pupils when they come to the tomb to grieve and lament.

"I shall stay here to tell them that he lives."

"But we just saw your Brothers carry his dead body from this garden!"

"Even so, the timeless one still lives who used that mortal form as garment and external veil, the while he needed such, in order to reveal the Spirit's life to those who only see external veil and garment."

"If your words reveal the truth, then tell us, too, where we ourselves can find that living one, because you speak of him as of a being one would feel compelled to search for, even to the ends of the earth."

"Within yourselves!"

And as we looked at one another, wondering about the meaning of those words, the white-robed messenger had gone from us unnoticed; and our calling after him was left without an answer.

Only in later years did light inform our understanding; we then beheld the living one and comprehended his celestial teachings. And from that moment forth he was *in us*.

At the time the white-clad figure had been speaking with the witnesses to answer their questions, two of his Brothers were waiting, in a mountain gorge not far away, for the arrival of the other four who brought their Brother's body.

While waiting, the two had gathered wood and kindling, raising it to build a heap on which the body could be laid to rest.

Seeing the carriers approach, they hurried toward them to give help, because the four were tired.

Stirred to their depths, in wordless veneration, the six then raised the body of their Brother, whose mighty work was finished, onto the gathered wood, committing it to the flame, which had been struck from a stone

Viewed from a distance, one barely could detect a fading trace of smoke that slowly drifted toward the mountains as the early rays of dawn began to color the summits of the hills.

The truly risen one himself, however, had wanted everything fulfilled that way; and what his Brothers did was all performed according to his will.

His mortal form's decaying elements were not to shroud the Resurrection he had created for himself within the souls of those he called his own.

Unfettered now and free of everything that was not of the Spirit in his nature, he only knew himself in his eternal being's spiritual form— no longer conscious of the wrongs his earthly body had endured.

His own self having risen from the dead, in his eternal spiritual body, he has been present ever since those days within the spiritual aura of this earth, abiding in transfigured life, in very truth the Resurrection unto all who prove themselves in active life as true disciples of his teachings.

And in this way he is alive among his own, even as he once had promised, "unto the end of the world."

CHAPTER FIVE
COMMUNION

Having arrived at the house of the sages who are guardians of light, I began to knock at the portal as someone who rightfully claims admittance—but no one came who might have opened.

Thus, sadness overwhelmed my soul and drained of strength I fell asleep before the threshold.

When, after harrowing, chaotic dreams, I finally awakened, there stood a man in front of me, leading a beast of burden laden with baskets of woven rushes, filled with rings of freshly baked bread.

"What made you come here, stranger?" asked the man addressing me.

"Do you not know this gate will not unlock itself to anyone who has not crossed its threshold first by passing over from within?"

I then replied, "If what you say is true, I am undone; for I have come from far away because the Master bade me take this path to those residing in this house, that I might be admitted to enter their community."

The man now said to me,

"I, too, belong to those who dwell within this house and in my spirit I am well aware of your desire; yet even so I tell you: None has ever entered through this portal unless he first had died.

"If, after his death, he finds himself alive again within this house, he then may freely leave and enter as he wishes.

"If, then, you are prepared to die in order to be one of us, let this beast of burden carry you across the threshold as a corpse."

"How could I then not also want to die," I answered him, "if, as you say, I cannot otherwise become a member of your circle?

"End my life this instant to make me cross the threshold; because I know that on that portal's other side my death shall have an end.

"Did you not likewise die one day to get across the threshold? And yet you stand before me now alive!"

"Let all be done to you according to your will," the man replied and no sooner had he spoken than I could feel my body growing lifeless and all knowledge of my conscious self dissolve in shudders.

Before I grew aware, however, that I had altogether left my body, I thought it strange to find myself again as one among the rings of bread that filled the woven baskets on the beast of burden.

I wanted to call out, but had no voice.

It was as if one tried to shout in some nightmarish dream, but lacks the power.

I sought to escape, but the bread that had become my body would not move.

At that point my self-awareness faded; and in this state one must have taken me into the house and put me on the table, where soon I found myself again, with other food, placed before the bowl of the eldest of the sages.

I did not have to lie this way for long, however, still in the grip of dark oppressive dreams, before I heard the voice of the eldest of the sages, saying,

"Sanctified and blessed be this bread, which would become the Spirit's living food!

"Forever let it henceforth serve the hidden Godhead as nourishment within the worlds of the Eternal."

Having said these words, he broke in half the bread I had become, and I could feel the tear through all my body, as if my human mortal form were being torn apart.

Trembling with pain I now felt sure of my annihilation; and thus I longed for death as liberating freedom; for I no longer could escape the power into whose hands I willingly had offered up my being.

The eldest continued breaking the bread into more and more pieces so that he could share it with all of his brothers; and in each of these shares my own self was alive.

Again my conscious self-awareness was engulfed by night.

But this darkness did not long encumber me; for soon I felt surrounded by a clarity I had not known before, however bright the light had been in which the Master once had taught me to discern events in each of the three worlds, before he made me undertake the long ascent to reach the dwelling of the sages.

And suddenly I also felt myself again within a human body and hardly could believe that I no longer was a ring of bread, like those in form that I had seen inside the woven baskets carried by the beast of burden at the portal.

And, still amazed, I spoke—yet what I said were words the eldest of the sages uttered.

His body had become my own; nor could my spirit be divorced from his.

But when the sages, his spiritual brothers, became aware of what had taken place, their spokesman, whom I recognized as the man who earlier had found me at the portal, said,

"Let there be jubilance in our midst, knowing a new brother has been born among us! And you, the eldest of our circle, who forges the eternal chain of Luminaries, have made your hammer close the open ring to give the chain another link."

"It is even as you say.

"Your words acknowledge my arrival."

Thus I spoke, but through the mouth of the eldest of the sages.

"As food I came to you, that I might be reborn within your spirit.

"Now, however, do not keep my own garb from me any longer, that I need not be here among you in another's guise, while I myself remain in hiding."

Responding to my words, the sages left their places at the tables and, following the eldest, with whose spirit mine was now united, they all went out and gathered in front of the portal.

Lying there, however, was my earthly body, lifeless and rigid as in death.

Now the eldest bent down over it and, speaking in a whisper, more like breathing on that body, said the words,

"You are I!

"Render, henceforth, service to your will in me, and to my will in you, in this your earthly garment!

"You now are born as food to nourish the life of the Light whose bounty feeds all."

When the eldest had spoken these words, I felt how my sensations departed from his earthly body, while my spirit's life remained as one with his.

At the same time, however, my consciousness awoke again inside the body wherein I had arrived before the portal; yet now that body was no longer quite the same it once had been.

Something in it had become transformed; and now I could discern, within my body's inner self, the three existing worlds—the realms of matter, soul, and Spirit—as clearly as I earlier had only seen the outer world by means of the external eye.

As soon as I had risen, however, the sages welcomed me with boundless joy, as someone is received who had been long expected.

And as they guided him who had become a new link in their midst, and led him through the portal into the inner halls of the house, the eldest, divinely enraptured, began to sing a chant whose words arranged themselves as follows:

"Live serving love to nourish the Light. Enlightened as teacher, bring light to the world."

And the chorus of the sages, who henceforth were to be my brothers, responded with this antiphon,

"Learn to perceive your radiance in light! Live serving love, bringing light to the world."

But in my soul I now possessed the spiritual knowledge of all who were around me.

I found them all as one within me, and had in each of them attained the consciousness that earlier I had known only in myself.

Part Three

THE WILL TO JOY

GOD IS ALIVE IN JOY,
NOT IN THE GLOOM OF GRIEF.

MINDS ENSLAVED BY GRIEF
CONCEIVED THE "SUFFERING" GOD
TO OFFER HIM THEIR WORSHIP.

BUT YOU SHOULD FORCE
YOUR GRIEF INTO YOUR SERVICE
THAT IT MAY TURN INTO A
HELPER OF YOUR WILL TO JOY!

CHAPTER ONE

TO ALL WHO STRIVE TOWARD TIMELESS LIGHT

Do not bar your way to God with questions!

Let those who live devoid of God and all who worship idols argue whether God exists.

Your reasons are well founded when you doubt that God is indiscernible.

We, by contrast, know for certain that God will not respond to anyone who questions his existence.

We know that God withdraws from noisy quarrels and debates.

Who, however, can be sure that he would not discern God's voice if he but learned to hear God's language?

What that demands above all else is silence!

All creative powers work in silence.

Devote a shrine to silence in yourself that God may make your house his dwelling and become your friend!

THESE WORDS would guide your soul to all-surpassing silence.

For a while, we here shall speak to you about the human being.

In seeking God, the human being must become the point of your departure, lest God remain a stranger to your soul forever.

We shall not search for God in the contrition of the heart, because it was God's will to joy that gave us life.

To help you, we shall not here inquire after God by asking questions; for even in a question barely whispered one hears the clamor of inherent doubts.

We teach, instead, how God is found in silence —and in the will to joy.

TO ALL WHO STRIVE TOWARD TIMELESS LIGHT

From those who cry for God with fear and anguish in their hearts we purposely shall turn away; how else could we attain with you the realm of inmost silence?

We need to be alone with the perceptive soul we seek to guide to silence.

Those who would discern the voice of God must first have learned how to discern their own eternal self.

That self must seek to answer its own being.

It must transform itself into a voiceless question and give its answer as a silent deed.

A self that in this way can answer its own questions is one with whom we can attain the realm where timeless silence reigns.

With such a self we can pursue the paths on which alone the voice of God is heard.

None but those who learned to know themselves can look upon the teachings that we here convey as being meant for them.

CHAPTER TWO

THE TEACHINGS ON JOY

ON THE SHORE of the ocean I saw a mother sitting with her child.

The child was playing in the sand with shells and colored pebbles.

All its play, however, consisted of choosing and rejecting.

ARE WE NOT ourselves like children playing such a game?

We choose and we reject, and in this way continue through the years and decades until the day arrives when we make ready to depart.

Are we not driven by the same desire that caused the child to play with shells and pebbles?

Here let as pause a moment and reflect.

From this viewpoint we shall see the rising of the sun.

Why should we race around the globe at night, behind the sun, and try to overtake it?

Already we have found the human being who to himself is both the question and the answer.

Choosing and rejecting define that being's active life.

You never will find mortal man engaged in anything besides.

To be sure, you will be given many cogent reasons if you ask why people act the way they do.

But human beings rarely more deceive themselves than when they seek to probe the final motives of their actions.

From deep within the same eternal wellspring rise alike the force that moves the child to play and the effective impulse driving every deed.

The final cause in either case, found at the deepest level, remains the will to joy.

To countless mysteries it holds the key.

All your thoughts and actions constitute your "shells" and "colored stones."

According to what you are worth you either will reject or choose.

Soon you will discover that much deserves to be rejected because it fails to serve enduring joy.

Nonetheless, you gather many colored pebbles into heaps and, for a while, your eye delights in their appearance.

In the end, however, you lose interest in merely playing.

You learn to judge and to distinguish values.

What now you want to find are precious stones and real pearls, not merely empty shells and colored pebbles.

At first your courage falters.

You see how your discernment has caused your erstwhile joy to die.

Dispirited, your eye drifts without hope across the sand.

But look—among the pebbles there gleams a shiny flash!

Hurriedly you cast aside your colored stones to make that shiny object yours.

You thus have found your first authentic jewel.

As of this day you have grown wise.

You will no longer find your joy in hoarding pebbles, which only glisten while the waters keep them moist.

From this day on you will abandon many things your eye may find attractive and search for only those rare gems whose radiance lasts forever.

Such is what the will to joy demands:

> Joy without dejection;
> Joy without ceasing;
> Joy without end!

BUT NOW YOUR question will be, "If these teachings state the truth, what is the source of grief?"

To which my answer is: Grief must exist as the condition and prerequisite of joy.

THE TEACHINGS ON JOY

All life within the universe embraces polar opposites.

Small and great; low and high; grief and joy; falsehood and truth; weakness and strength—such are the elements that generate all being.

If grief did not exist, then joy as well could not assert its being. To be sure, all separating and dividing causes grief, but separation and division needs must be if joy is to reveal itself in all the forms its infinitely differentiated energy requires, whose workings are the source that nourishes all life.

Your will to joy, however, shall make you see that grief is, finally, deception and thus its value shall diminish in your eyes.

Joy and grief depend upon each other and yet are constantly at war, without their ever being able to make peace.

Joy and grief alike would dominate your energies.

Both joy and grief compete for your esteem.

The more you treasure joy, the less you value grief, until at last it shall become a willing servant of your joy.

THE BOOK ON THE ROYAL ART

I SURELY DO NOT counsel you to keep your distance from all hardship, like a coward.

The will to joy would often guide the human soul through gloomy depths of fate to reach the heights of radiant light.

There is no victory without a battle.

To fight a battle means inflicting wounds, as well as to sustain them.

Grief will come into your life through others and you in turn become the cause of others' grief.

Beware, however, in your will to joy of finding joyful even wounds you must inflict!

You are to chain your grief wherever it would make you suffer to no purpose.

When grief would challenge you to battle, however, attaining victory must be your goal.

All grief is, in reality, deception.

All grief shall one day vanish in the light of truth.

Grief as such does not endure.

Joy alone is everlasting; for it is rooted in eternity.

All grief is your opponent and your foe.

You must subdue and force your grief to serve you that joy be granted freedom and assert its rule.

But never must you hate your grief!

Hate is the banner of impotence.

The will to joy, by contrast, shall make you learn the victor's love.

The will to joy shall lighten all your burdens.

You thus have life's most powerful creative energy beside you.

Even those who seek to increase grief are secretly pursuing joy.

Their will to joy, while closely fettered, even so remains the wellspring of their energy.

The will to joy lies at the root of every action.

The will to joy engenders all of life.

Choose yourself, then, whether, as a victim of deception having battled for a lie, you would remain a thrall to grief, or conquer it and prove yourself its victor.

You cannot lose that battle, except by showing fear in face of grief.

The will to joy would make you perfect as a victor free of fear.

You find the will to joy at work throughout creation.

The will to joy requires form and measure, that love may give it life.

Love is the drive that would unite all things divided.

Only love can conquer hatred and make it serve your will.

Love unites all elements in opposition.

Love is the might through which alone the will to joy gains power to engender joy.

The will to joy embodies male polarity; it needs its female counterpart, the might of love, to give it birth.

Devoid of love, the will to joy would be condemned eternally to wander without rest.

Only love bestows on it both aim and purpose.

Love engenders harmony between opposed polarities.

Love assigns to all things small their place among things great.

Love unifies both things of value and devoid of worth in all-embracing harmony, according to eternal laws.

It values even what is lacking worth, mindful of the values it must serve; for there is no dimension of Reality where worth or worthlessness exist in isolation.

Although unlike in rank, neither would be found without the other.

All things that seek to grow must strive to integrate both things possessing and devoid of worth.

All forms of life have need of unifying unlike parts through love.

Only thus can grow what shall endure.

Witnessing that human beings die, you ask, "Where is now a thing that shall endure?"

Instead, you ought to ask, "Where is here a thing that shall no longer be?"

I saw my dearest loved ones die, yet I could not discover anything that ceased to be.

Consider what remained of all who ever lived on earth and you will simply find a new configuration of component elements, even to the limits your external eye is able to observe.

Who would ever show you anything that ceased to be in realms your mortal eye cannot perceive?

The very sphere your mortal eye cannot discern today you were unable to perceive even at the time your loved ones were still present to your senses.

Formerly, your senses merely made you conscious of a particular reality of whose existence only its effects on your perception gave you proof.

Thus, if you now believe that the reality has ceased to be which you were sure to have existed when its presence still affected your perception, you truly are your mortal senses' hapless slave.

Eᴠᴇɴ ᴛʜᴇ traditional rites of mourning for the dead are lastly rooted in the will to joy, which feels its lack of power to bring back what it had once enjoyed.

Such mourning would perfidiously deceive you if it destroyed your faith in the continued life of those whom now your physical eye no longer can perceive because it is not capable of seeing anything but objects that external senses apprehend.

It is yourself you ought to mourn, for you allowed your mind to be deceived.

Only that which once had touched your body's senses you had thought to be a person's real being.

Now you are reminded that the fleeting joy experienced through another's earthly presence differs quite profoundly from the joy inspired by that being's timeless self.

You now must learn to recognize that the domain of visible phenomena is but the temporal effect of causes whose reality you cannot see.

All ultimate Reality will manifest itself from realms that are not seen.

If you would find the human being's true reality, you only will discover it in the domain that is not seen, and then by virtue of your own invisible reality.

Much within the world you see you may believe as being true to its appearance; still, you should not trust that everything is truly as it seems.

You need to learn to look upon your visible reality as the material counterpart of your invisible existence.

We could not here on earth experience our presence but for the will that, in our nature, strives toward the external realm to manifest itself by means of mortal senses.

Will—invisibly at work and visibly made manifest—is unified within us in the world of time.

We still do not approach the state the Spirit's law demands at which the two polarities are permanently unified.

> Being liberated from excess,
> finding one's deficiencies made whole:

such, in truth, is the event of "death," which disengages our unseen essence from the visible domain.

No more confined by visible forms of matter, we even then shall be alive and active—visible in a dimension that is seen—each of us a self that is complete, but now endowed with consciousness by the eternal, all-embracing source that is completeness in itself.

Because their "outer" world became an "inner" realm, while your own life "within" still struggles with your world "outside," you cannot find a way that leads to those you call "the dead."

Even though there is a path that leads to where they are, very few in any generation are able to pursue it without risk.

That path begins in the external world and passes through the inmost halls of nature before its goal is reached.

Whoever means to enter it must let his own light show the way, lest he should lose himself within the labyrinths through which he has to wander.

Darkness and confusion will surround him here until at last he will himself fall prey to their destructive powers.

Insanity is then the outcome of his quest.

All who can pursue that path protected from all danger—purposely avoid it.

Each of them could vouch for the truth of my words.

You can scarcely recognize yourself within your inner world; how could you there expect to apprehend the distant voices of departed souls?

On the other hand, it is completely useless to search for evidence within the "outer" world to prove what only can be found within the innermost dimension of the "inner" realm.

ETERNAL LIFE embraces rest and action.

Rest and action alternate eternally, like tides of ebb and flow, within the timeless sea of cosmic emanation.

Eternal rest would truly be death everlasting.

Eternal action would be true damnation.

Rest and action, unified in joy, are life eternal lived in bliss.

You wrongly understand your feelings if you believe that what you long for is "eternal rest."

What your spirit truly longs for is eternal joy embracing rest and action.

Joy is human intuition of divine perfection.

That is why you ought to let the will to joy grow powerful within you.

You cannot ever long too much for joy.

And never can you lose again what here and now you will be granted of enduring joy.

Everywhere has nature posted signs along her roads.

Mortals blindly frolic past them, like children dancing when they play.

You ought to learn more carefully to heed those signs!

You still are seeking carnal pleasures and let yourself be driven by desires, while only joy shall lead you to eternal life.

God abides in joy!

Joy is radiant light!

Carnal pleasures and desire burn and smolder in the dark.

The will to joy in truth is will to God.

Recognize yourself as what you are:

You had existed as a dormant will before the time that one of the polarities within your nature desired incarnation in the world of matter.

Even now you are a will that lives in dreams.

Yet step by step you shall become a will that is awake; until one day your lucid will shall, as a living force, pervade all elements within you in clarity and joy.

All tablets, scrolls, and books of law are rooted in the will to joy.

You are yourself that will to joy; and thus you only follow your own law when you resolve to know yourself in joy, and through that joy, in God.

Everything effecting timeless joy will serve you.

THE TEACHINGS ON JOY

Everything that will not serve enduring joy must do you harm.

You are the judge of your own actions and your decisions are your deeds.

You have the power to "condemn" yourself for ages, or you can raise yourself to share the timeless "bliss of heaven" through your works.

Yet no matter how much time you stray in error, in the end you shall be forced to follow your own law, even though this might not be for aeons.

The day that you shall know yourself you will awaken in the Godhead's light.

Your impulse now is still to strive into some distant emptiness of sterile nothing.

Your sight is still directed toward some outer sphere where you are searching for a thousand goals you sense "out there."

In the end, however, you will come to recognize that only you yourself should be the goal you ought to reach, inspired by the will to joy that you afford yourself.

Within your hands you hold the power that will either "bind" or "loose" your spirit's life.

You now are not yet conscious of the power you possess.

You still expect to find within the outer world what only shall reveal itself within.

But you shall apprehend the world "without" and that "within" as being one when you at last shall know yourself enlightened by the will to joy.

For years you have been taught that only consciousness of guilt, self-condemnation, and contrition could ever bring you close to God.

You had accepted and believed these teachings and now you are afraid to set out on the quest that takes you to yourself and to your God.

Do not fear anything, however, except what seeks to fill your mind with fear.

The might of joy shall make you fearless on your path as soon as your own will imbues your being with the will to joy.

The will to joy will let you partake of eternal life.

The will to joy will let your living God reveal himself within you.

And in the will to joy shall God be one with you for all eternity.

You then shall comprehend that nothing more than gloomy idols once had sought to keep you from the joy that you afford yourself—the final wellspring of your will to joy.

You then shall recognize that what had barred your way to knowing joy was—fear.

Experience then will show you that only when you are yourself the source that grants you joy can you be certain to possess your being.

Now, as a gift, in sacred joy eternally bestowed upon yourself, you shall abide in joy forever.

EPILOGUE

Knowledge that is kept so secret
by the circle of the very few
with whom I am united in the Spirit as their brother,
yet who feel bound by bonds of blood
to grant of it no more than sparing insight
even to severely tested pupils,
after long and manifold ordeals—
such knowledge I received permission to disclose
to everyone who comprehends my words.

All objections seeking to inhibit such disclosure
were disarmed;
in mindfulness that
even what has been revealed,
continues to be veiled
to every eye that has not learned to see.

But purposely I parted ways
with Western modes of thinking,
which recognize as "real"
only what the brain regards as such.

For as I am conjoined
to order everlasting,
the laws that I obey
transcend the bounds of time.

REMINDER

"Yet here I must point out again that if one would derive the fullest benefit from studying the books I wrote to show the way into the Spirit, one has to read them in the original; even if this should require learning German.

"Translations can at best provide assistance in helping readers gradually perceive, even through the spirit of a different language, what I convey with the resources of my mother tongue."

From "Answers to Everyone" (1933), *Gleanings*. Bern: Kobersche Verlagsbuchhandlung, 1990

Other Works by Bô Yin Râ published in English translation:

Bô Yin Râ:
An Introduction to His Works

Contents: Preface. About My Books. Concerning My Name. In My Own Behalf. Essential Distinction. Résumé. Comments on the Cycle <Hortus Conclusus> and the Related Works. Brief Biography of Bô Yin Râ. The Works of Bô Yin Râ.

The Kober Press, 2004, 117 pages, paperback. ISBN 0-915034-10-7

This book presents a summary of the essential features that set the author's works on final things apart from the innumerable publications, old and new, that seek to answer questions which thinking minds have asked in every generation. Traditionally, such answers draw upon beliefs, accepted faith, and speculative thought, culminating in systems of religion and philosophy. Rarely have solutions rested on objective insights into the dynamic structure of reality, embracing both its physical and spiritual dimensions. But in addition to providing such direct descriptions of these aspects of reality, the author's books are helpful guides that let the readers gradually develop their inherent faculties so that they may experience this reality themselves. For readers having sensed the nature of this ultimate experience the concepts "spirit," "soul, "eternal life," and "God" are then no longer merely abstract notions based on hope and faith, but have become realities that form the human being's timeless essence, even as they underlie all aspects of creation.

In the first chapter of this *Introduction* the author discusses the origin and purpose of his books; how they should be used; for whom they are intended, and what their application may accomplish. Here he also stresses that his writings neither are opposed to, nor written to support, any particular religious creed, even though the followers of all persuasions may benefit from what they have to offer to all who seek to know.

The following chapter sheds light on the author's name and explains why his books are published under this spiritual proper name, which is not an arbitrary pseudonym, invented for the purpose of effective self-illumination, but expresses, in phonetic equivalents, the essence of his nature.

In the final chapter he corrects a number of misunderstandings of his books and person, typically prompted by hasty judgments, hearsay, or prejudice. Here he also touches on the common source of all authentic spiritual disclosures and stresses that objective insights into that dimension ought to be distinguished from the subjective mystical visions found in the different forms of religion.

The Book on the Living God

Contents: Word of Guidance. "The Tabernacle of God is with Men." The "Mahatmas" of Theosophy. Meta-Physical Experiences. The Inner Journey. The En-Sof. On Seeking God. On Leading an Active Life. On "Holy Men" and "Sinners." The Hidden Side of Nature. The Secret Temple. Karma. War and Peace. The Unity among Religions. The Will to Find Eternal Light. Mankind's Higher Faculties of Knowing. On Death. On the Spirit's Radiant Substance. The Path toward Perfection. On Everlasting Life. The Spirit's Light Dwells in the East. Faith, Talismans, and Images of God. The Inner Force in Words. A Call from Himavat. Giving Thanks. Epilogue.

The Kober Press, 1991. 333 pages, paperback. ISBN 0-915034-03-4

This work is the central volume of the author's *Enclosed Garden*, a cycle of thirty-two books that let the reader gain a clear conception of the structure, laws, and nature of eternal life, and its reflections here on earth. The present work sheds light on the profound distinction between the various ideas and images of "God" that human faith has molded through the ages —as objects for external worship—and the eternal *spiritual reality*, which human souls are able to experience, even in this present life. How readers may attain this highest of all earthly goals; what they must do, and what avoid; and how their mortal life can be transformed into an integrated part of their eternal being, are topics fully treated in these pages.

What sets this author's works on spiritual life apart from other writings on the subject is their objective clarity, which rests upon direct perception of eternal life and its effects on human life on earth. Such perception is only possible, as he points out, if the observer's *spiritual* senses are as thoroughly developed to perceive realities of timeless life, as earthly senses need to be in order to experience *physical* existence. Given that authentic insights gathered in this way have always been extremely rare, they rank among the most important writings of their time, conveying knowledge of enduring worth that otherwise would not become accessible.

The Book on Life Beyond

Contents: Introduction. The Art of Dying. The Temple of Eternity and the World of Spirit. The Only Absolute Reality. What Should One Do?

The Kober Press, 2002. 161 pages, paperback. ISBN 0-915034-11-5.

This book explains why life "beyond" is not so much a different and wholly other life, but rather the continuation of the self-same life we live on earth. The difference between the two dimensions lies chiefly in the organs of perception through which the same reality of life is individually experienced. On earth we know that life through our mortal senses, in life beyond it is perceived through spiritual faculties, which typically awaken after death. At that transition, the human consciousness, which usually is unprepared for the event, is at a loss and finds itself confused by the beliefs and concepts of its former mortal life. As a result, the new arrival faces certain dangers; for, owing to these mental prejudices, the person is unable to distinguish between perceptions of objective truth and the alluring phantom "heavens" generated by misguided faith on earth.

To help perceptive readers form correct and realistic expectations, that they may one day reach the other shore with confidence and without fear, this book provides trustworthy guidance into spiritual life, its all-pervading structure, laws, and inner nature. Given the unbreakable connection between our actions here on earth and their effects on life beyond, the book advises how this present life may best prepare the reader for the life that is to come.

The Book on Human Nature

Contents: Introduction. The Mystery Enshrouding Male and Female. The Path of the Female. The Path of the Male. Marriage. Children. The Human Being of the Age to Come. Epilogue. A Final Word.

The Kober Press, 2000, 168 pages, paperback, ISBN 0-915034-07-7

Together with *The Book on the Living God* and *The Book on Life Beyond*, *The Book on Human Nature* forms a trilogy containing guidelines toward a new and more objective understanding of both physical and spiritual realities, and of the human being's origin and place within these two dimensions of creation.

The Book on Human Nature at the outset shows the need to draw a clear distinction between the timeless spiritual component present in each mortal human, and the material creature body in which the spiritual essence is embodied during mortal life. The former, indestructible and timeless, owing to its being born of spiritual substance, represents the truly human element in what is known as mortal man. The latter, physical, contingent, and subject to decay and death, is no more than the temporary instrument the spiritual being uses to express itself in physical existence. Given that the spiritual and animal components within human nature manifest inherently discordant aspects of reality, they typically contend for domination of the total individual. Experience shows that in this conflict the animal component with its ruthless drives and instincts clearly proves the stronger.

To help the reader gain a realistic understanding of the human being's spiritual and physical beginnings, by way of concepts more in keeping with humanity's advances in every discipline of natural science, the book explains, to the extent that metaphysical events can be conveyed through language, the timeless origin and source of every human's spiritual descent. It likewise shows that the material organism, now considered mankind's primal ancestor, existed long before it was to serve the spiritual individuation as its earthly tool. In this context the author points out that the traditional creation story, such as it has survived, is not simply an archaic myth, invented at a time that lacked the benefits of modern knowledge, but instead preserves, in lucid images and symbols, a truthful view of actual events. Events, however, that did not happen merely once, at the beginning of creation, but are a process that continues even now, and will recur until this planet can no longer nurture human life.

Even so, the principal intention of the present work, as well as of the author's other expositions of reality, is not so much to offer readers a new, reliable cosmology, but rather to encourage them to rediscover and awaken the spiritual nature in themselves, and thus to live their present and their future life as fully conscious, truly human beings.

The Book on Happiness

Contents: Prelude. Creating Happiness as Moral Duty. "I" and "You". Love. Wealth and Poverty. Money. Optimism. Conclusion.

The Kober Press, 1994. 127 pages, paperback. ISBN 0-915034-04-2.

Sages and philosophers in every age and culture have speculated on the nature, roots, and attributes of happiness, and many theories have sought to analyze this enigmatic subject. In modern times, psychology has joined the search for concrete answers with its own investigations, which frequently arrive at findings that support established views. Still, the real essence of true happiness remains an unsolved riddle.

In contrast to traditional approaches, associating happiness with physical events, the present book points to the spiritual source from which all human happiness derives, both in life on earth and in the life to come. Without awareness of this nonmaterial fundament, one's understanding of true happiness is bound to be deficient.

The author shows that real happiness is neither owing to blind chance, nor a capricious gift of luck, but rather the creation of determined human will. It is an inner state that must be fostered day by day; for real happiness, as it is here defined, is "the contentment that creative human will enjoys in its creation." How that state may be created and sustained, in every aspect of this life, the reader can discover in this book.

The Book on Love

Contents: Introduction. The Greatest of Compassion's Mediators. On Love's Primordial Fire. Light of Liberation. On Love's Creative Power.

The Kober Press,. 2005. 148 pages, paperback. ISBN 978-0-915034-12-3

Love, properly understood, is not merely, as the author explains, a human sentiment of varying degrees of intensity, inspired by particular objects and, like all feelings, subject to continuous change. Love is, instead, the highest of creation's elemental powers, giving life to and sustaining all dimensions of reality. The human sentiment called "love" is but a faint reflection of that cosmic force and ought to be distinguished clearly from its distant source.

Earthly love in all its forms is typically aroused by the desire of possession for an object. Celestial love, by contrast, is a spiritual energy that manifests itself beyond and free of all desire, independent of external objects. Human beings can partake of the celestial form of love, which then transforms their temporal existence by virtue of their timeless life, and thus will make them more than simply "sounding brass and tinkling cymbals."

In its initial chapter the book sheds light on the historical facts surrounding the life and teachings of the unprecedented figure of Jesus of Nazareth, who, more perfectly than anyone before or since, embodied love's celestial force in word and deed. Empowered by that highest form of love he found the strength to change this planet's spiritual aura in his final hour and freed all human beings of good will from ancient bondage.

The Book on Solace

Contents: On Grief and Finding Solace. Lessons One Can Learn from Grief. On Follies to Avoid. On the Comforting Virtue of Work. On Solace in Bereavement.

The Kober Press, 1996. 126 pages, paperback. ISBN 0-915034-05-0.

In this book the author shows how sorrow, pain, and grief, although inevitable burdens of this present life, can and ought to be confronted and confined within the narrow borders of necessity. Considered from the spiritual perspective, all suffering experienced on this earth is the inexorable consequence of mankind's having willfully abandoned its given state of harmony within the Spirit, a deed that also ruined the perfection of material nature. Although the sum of grief thus brought upon this planet is immense, human beings needlessly expand and heighten its ferocity by foolishly regarding grief as something noble and refined, if not, indeed, a token of God's "grace."

Understanding pain objectively, as a defect confined to physical existence, which, even in exceptional cases, is but an interlude in every mortal's timeless life, allows the reader to perceive its burdens in a clearer light, and thus more patiently to bear it with resolve.

While suffering, through human fault, remains the tragic fate of physical creation, the highest source of solace, which helps the human soul endure its pain and sorrow, continually sends its comfort from the Spirit's world to all who seek it in themselves. How readers may discover and draw solace from that inner source the present book will show them.

The Wisdom of St. John

Contents: Introduction. The Master's Image. The Luminary's Mortal Life. The Aftermath. The Missive. The Authentic Doctrine. The Paraclete. Conclusion.

The Kober Press, 1975. 92 pages, clothbound. ISBN 0-915034-01-8.

This exposition of the Fourth Gospel is not a scholarly analysis discussing the perplexing riddles of this ancient text. It is, instead, a nondogmatic reconstruction of the actual events recorded in that work, whose author wanted to present the truth about the Master's life and teachings; for the image propagated by the missionaries of the new religion often was in conflict with the facts. The present book restores the context of essential portions of the unknown author's secret missive, which the first redactors had corrupted, so that its contents would support the other gospels.

Written by a follower of John, the "beloved disciple," its purpose was to disavow the "miracles" the other records had ascribed to the admired teacher. His record also is unique in that it has preserved the substance of some letters by the Master's hand, addressed to that favorite pupil. Those writings are reflected in the great discourses which set this gospel text apart and lend it its distinctive tone.

Given the historic impact of the man presented in this work, an accurate conception of his life and message will not only benefit believers of the faith established in his name, but also may explain to others what his death in fact accomplished for mankind.

The Meaning of this Life

Contents: A Call to the Lost. The Iniquity of the Fathers. The Highest Goal. The "Evil" Individual. Summons from the World of Light. The Benefits of Silence. Truth and Verities. Conclusion.

The Kober Press, 1998, 126 pages, paperback. ISBN 0-915034-06-9.

This book addresses the most common questions people tend to ask at times when circumstances in their daily lives awaken their awareness of the many unsolved riddles that surround the human being here on earth. To be sure, philosophy and teachings of religion have offered answers to such questions through the ages, but as these often draw on speculation, or require blind belief, they can no longer truly satisfy the searching mind of our time.

It is against this background that the present book will guide its readers to a firmer ground of understanding, resting on objective insights and experience. From this solid vantage, readers may survey their own existence and its purpose with assurance.

As this book explains, the key to comprehending the meaning of this present life is, first, the insight that this life is but the consequence of causes in the Spirit's world and, thus, has of itself no meaning other than that fact. And, secondly, the recognition that material life is ultimately meaningless if human beings fail to give it meaning: by virtue of pursuing goals whose blessings shall endure. The nature of the highest goal that mortals can pursue provides the substance also of the present book.

Spirit and Form

Contents: The Question. Outer World and Inner Life. At Home and at Work. Forming One's Joy. Forming One's Grief. The Art of Living Mortal Life.

The Kober Press, 2000. 108 pages, paperback. ISBN 0-915034-07-7

The underlying lesson of this book is that all life in the domain of spiritual reality, from the highest to the lowest spheres, reveals itself as lucid order, form, and structure. Spirit, the all-sustaining radiant *substance* of creation, is in itself the final source and pattern of all perfect form throughout its infinite dimensions. Nothing, therefore, can exist within, or find admittance to, the Spirit's inner worlds that is devoid of the perfection, harmony, and structure necessarily prevailing in these spheres.

Given that this present life is meant to serve the human being as an effective preparation for regaining the experience of spiritual reality, this life must needs be lived in ways that are consistent with the principles that govern spiritual reality; in other words, ought to be lived according to the structure, laws, and inner forms of that reality. To show the reader how this present life receives enduring form, which then is able to survive this mortal state, the book sheds light on crucial aspects of this physical existence and advises how these may be formed to serve one's spiritual pursuits.

Worlds of Spirit
A Sequence of Cosmic Perspectives

Contents: Preface. The Ascent. The Return. Reviews of Creation. Epilogue.

Illustrations: *Emanation. In Principio erat Verbum. Lux in Tenebris. Te Deum Laudamus. Space and Time. Primal Generation. Seeds of Future Worlds. Emerging Worlds. Birth of the External Cosmos. Labyrinth. Desire for External Form. Astral Luminescence. Sodom. Inferno. De Profundis. Revelation. Illumination. Fulfillment. Victory. Himavat.*

The Kober Press, 2002. 96 pages, 20 full-color illustrations, hardcover. ISBN 0-915034-09-3.

If all the books of Bô Yin Râ, objectively considered, are unparalleled in the extensive literature on subjects touching final things—in that their author did not publish speculations based on faith or thought, but gave the reader fact-based insights into spiritual reality—the volume *Worlds of Spirit* occupies a special place even among these thirty-two unprecedented works; for in this book he integrated twenty reproductions of his paintings, representing *spiritual perspectives*, to illustrate selected aspects of his text.

While the works of the *Hortus Conclusus* cycle constitute the first authentic, comprehensive exposition of metaphysical realities, the paintings in this volume represent, in turn, the first objective visual renditions of spiritual dimensions in their dynamic figurations, colors, and inherent structure. Together with the written word—the book describes events experienced and perceived by an awakened human spirit—the images are meant to offer readers lucid concepts of nonphysical existence, and thereby to assist them in developing their own perceptive faculties.